The Twelve Universal Laws of Success

Nandanie
Dec '2006

Second Edition
Expanded

Herbert Harris

The LifeSkill® Institute, Inc.
P.O. Box 302
Wilmington, NC 28402

Seventh Printing: September 2006
Sixth Printing: January 2006
Fifth Printing: July 2005
Fourth Printing: February 2005
Third Printing: August 2004
Second Printing: May 2004
First Printing of the Second Edition, Expanded: January 2004

Published by:
LifeSkill® Institute, Inc.   SAN: 255-8440
P.O. Box 302
Wilmington, NC 28402
(800) 570-4009

Email: lifeskill@earthlink.net   *Website: www.lifeskillinstitute.org*

Library of Congress Cataloging-in-Publication Data

Harris, Herbert, 1944-
       The Twelve Universal Laws of Success / by
Herbert Harris
       p.   cm.
       ISBN 0-9748362-1-4 paperback edition
       ISBN 0-9748362-0-6 hardcover edition
BJ1611.2.H317 2004   158.1—dc21
Library of Congress Control Number: 2003115975

This edition distributed by

Executive Books
206 West Allen Street
Mechanicsburg, PA 17055

Printed in the United States of America

Table of Contents

Dedication

This Book is dedicated to my children:

Olivia Khera Harris	Sean Anthony McDuffie
Mark J. Brady	Sade Michelle McDuffie
Sean A. McDuffie, Jr.	Habeebah Rasheed
Hashim Rasheed	Alan Loar Williams
Ronald McDuffie	Charles Harrison
Jamie Ford	Ethan Robinson

And, to my Aunt **Lavinia E. Sneed**, whose love and guidance have given me a great appreciation for knowledge, hard work, and personal excellence.

With a special dedication to my daughter **Olivia Khera Harris**, whose simple, pure love, and affection, freely given, inspires me to be a better father.

And, to my friend, companion and partner **Sandra Spaulding Hughes**, whose advice, encouragement, and support made completing this book a reality.

To my editor **Mary Anne Mills**, whose editorial patience, skill, and recommendations made this a better book; and her daughter Katharine Elizabeth Stockett for patient understanding as her mother worked with the author.

To my friend **Valerie D. Wilson,** who believed in and encouraged an earlier version of this book.

To **Bishop James Utley, Jr.** and his wife **Pastor Maxine Utley** of the Love Center Church where many of the universal laws were shared with parents and members in 21st Century after-school programs.

To **Mary Alice Jervay Thatch**, publisher and editor of the Wilmington Journal, who published *Thoughts for Success*, the author's weekly newspaper column. Mary helped introduce the column to other newspapers accross the nation.

To **William Burton**, a motivational speaker and fellow traveler on the path to personal empowerment.

To **Tom Danley**, a friend, motivational speaker, founder, and president of Tom Danley's *"Tape of the Month"*. Tom has been diligent in bringing personal development to all who want to live a better life and be in business for themselves.

To **Ricky Young**, a motivated fellow traveler whose commitment to bringing personal growth to young people should be recognized.

Special Acknowledgements

Over years of personal study, I have been blessed to meet many extraordinary people who have shared their knowledge and experience to help me be a better person. A few of these very special people are:

Dr. Frederick J. Eikerenkkotter, better known as *Rev. Ike*, who shared unique insights into religion and metaphysics, and gave me an opportunity to work and study with him.

Dr. Eric Butterworth and The Unity, who provided weekly lessons of truth principles at Lincoln Center in New York City. These lessons were a great source of knowledge and inspiration.

Dr. Johnnie Colemon and Rev. Don Nedd, who gave me my first opportunity to speak before a large church.

Dr. Robert Schuller, whose TV ministry provided a spiritual continuity for me during my travels.

H.H. Brahmrishi Vishavatma Bawra Ji, whose teachings have been a source of enlightenment and healing.

Stuart, Sharon and Lauran Schultz, whose company, Marketing Programs, Inc. was very supportive during the writing of an earlier version of this book.

Rev. Ruth M. McDonald and the Miracle Church of Religious Science, who gave me lots of support, and numerous speaking opportunities.

Acknowledgements

Over my years of study, certain very special people have come into my life at critical times and shared their knowledge, time, and the example of their living. Some of these friends are:

Barry & Kim Ackle
Ashley R. Andrews, Esq.
Larry Barnett
Aldwin R. Brown
Tony Brown
Lynette Carrington
Rubi Celestine
Dr. Ernest Davis
Dr. Barbara Evans
Antoinette Franklin
Norman Frederick
John Harley
Burke Hedges
Cecelia Huffman
Ollie Jefferson
Khalil A. Malik
Jay Martin
Marie McCallum
Lea Leever Oldham
Barbara Nowell
Tiahmo Ra-uf
Anthony Robbins
Wynn Shafer
Earl & Dundie Shaw
David Smile
Peggy Stephens
Bob Tate
Mayor Michael R. White
John Wilson, III
Van Woods

Judi Allaire
Benjamin & Gale Armstead
Les Brown
Lorene Brown
Lester Bryant
Peter & Theresa Christian
Rev. Willie Cooper
Shy Dureaux
Edward F. Fordham, Esq.
George Fraser
Desmond Gibson
Cynthia Haywood
Michele Hill
Russell Hemphill
John H. Johnson
Marcelle A. Miranda
Michelle Posey Murphy
Minister Saba Mchunguzi
Nathan & Yvonne Oliver
John Raye
Terry Richardson, Esq.
Jerry Roebuck
David Sage
Dr. Milton Slaughter
Amir & Patricia Solomon
Bob & Lee Thomas
Eric Truxon
Anthony Welters
Dennis Windsor
Ali Yasin

Dr. George Butler
Marc Danaceau
Dr. Joe L. Dudley, Sr.
Stanley James
Bishop Linwood Nesbitt
Dee Perry
Susan Taylor
Iyanla Vanzant
Curtis Woods

Richard & Patricia Cliette
Suzanne DePasse
Peter Grear, Esq.
Estella Loar
Richard Parsons
Dr. Jewel Pookrum
Linda Upperman-Smith
Dr. Wyatt T. Walker
Garland Woods

Donn Ansel
Joyce Bass Binkley
Hollis B. Briggs, Jr.
Kevin "KB" Bryant
Dr. Denis Carter
Vanessa Cundiff
Jimmy Davis
Harry Forden, Sr.
Carolyn Gary
Michael & Kathleen Glancy
William Harrison
Tamm E. Hunt
Ron Love
Congressman Mike McIntyre
Dr. John Morris
Yvonne Pagan
Mayor Harper Peterson & Plunkett
Roy Roberts
Dr. Anne Russell
Melvin & Lela Thompson
Bertha B. Todd
Kenneth Weeden
Helen Worthy

Senator Patrick Ballantine
Nat Bost
Carl & Veronica Brown
Pamela Campbell-Dereef
Rev. Elijah and Dorothly Coleman
E. B. Davis, Sr.
Kenneth Davis
Carolyn S. Forte
Robert Gerlach
Lethia S. Hankins
Margaret Herring
Ali Kaazim
Johnny McCoy
Dr. Lee Monroe
Elsie & Sherad Ozaka
Linda Pearce
Benjamin Quattlebaum, II
Andre & Stacy Robinson
William "Billy" Sutton
Geraldine "Gerri" Tobias
Ernest & Theresa Walker
Olga Wheatley

Introduction

For Whom This Book Is Written

The Twelve Universal Laws of Success is written primarily for those who have done all right in life. Giving credit where credit is due, the fact that you are around at this time to read this book means that you have already succeeded where many of your generation have failed. You have survived.

You have pretty good health, and a decent job. However, from time to time, you've had more month at the end of your money. You probably own a house and a car. And, you've done your best to raise good children, who hopefully are, or will be self-sustaining, fairly soon.

At this point, you desire to do whatever it takes to get the knowledge, techniques, and associations that you need to create a better life for yourself. The fact that you are seriously reading this book—we call it, *"being on the path"*— is a clear indication that you are close to getting whatever you need, to obtaining the things you want.

Basically, all you need is a few key thoughts, some improvement and refinement of your habits and techniques, and one or two people who can assist or guide you on the path. This new insight, together with what you already know from experience, will guide you on your journey to the goals you wish to accomplish, the vision you desire to realize, and the person you want to become.

This book is a valuable guide to the young person who is just starting out in life on their own. It can provide valuable techniques, knowledge and understanding, which can help you avoid the pitfalls that always confront the novice. Learning to apply the information contained in this book will put you on the fast-track to true success and accomplishment at an early age. Those unique historical figures who made their mark on the world consciousness generally mastered the key principles set forth in this book at an early age.

Using This Book Most Effectively

Refresh Your Study Skills. One of the first and most important skills you must develop on your success journey is the skill of effective study. Without this skill, some otherwise dedicated students who are on the path become discouraged as a result of the difficulty they have in reading, studying and retaining information. One very effective technique to improve your study skills is the SQ3R Study Method.

The SQ3R Study Method

The SQ3R Study Method is a complete method which may be applied to any subject matter with excellent results. It may be used in reading an article, a book, or applied in learning the content of an entire course.

The first step in applying this method is SURVEY (S). Survey the material to be learned. Scan it in its entirety. Note the way the information is organized and its format. Pay special attention to the table of contents and chapter or topic headings. Look for any outlines or summaries of the material covered. Read them carefully. Familiarize yourself with the style of writing and the way information is organized. This survey should be done thoroughly and quickly. Make brief notes.

After surveying the material, write down QUESTIONS (Q) you expect to be answered by the material. These questions represent what you expect to learn.

The main purpose of surveying the material and writing relevant questions is to stimulate your mind and call forth what you already know about the material being studied. As you survey the material, silently instruct your mind to recall all that you know about the subject.

"Whatever I know about (this subject)
comes to the forefront of my thinking."

Next, READ (R1) the material thoroughly. As you read the material, think about the questions you expect to be answered. But, do not get sidetracked from your reading. Complete this reading from beginning to end. Make brief, concise notes of important information covered in your reading. Once you have completed the material, determine if all your questions have been answered. If not, why not? If so, write the answers down.

Now, REVIEW (R2) the material thoroughly. Focus on your notes and markings throughout the text. Make additional notes if necessary. Review the   important points and concentrate on learning them.

Finally, test yourself. RECITE (R3) orally what you have learned from your studies. Anything you cannot recall during this recitation exercise, you probably won't be able to recall at a later time. Recite the important points over and over until they are etched in your mind. Once you can recite the important points without looking at the material or at your notes, you have mastered this material once and for all.

Even if you do not totally understand some portions of the material, you will at the very least be able to recall it for future examination. Tell yourself that the information you recite is stored forever in your mind, and you have ready access to it in the future.

Use this method as you read this book. Apply it chapter by chapter. The results will astound you.

The Truth About Success

Success is generally defined as a favorable or satisfactory outcome or result. Whatever you do in your life, you get results. Whether or not those results are the ones you desired, is basically whether you succeeded or failed in your endeavors. Success is often defined as the gaining of wealth, fame, rank and so on. However, in the most general terms, *success is the the continuous realization of the outcomes or results you desire.*

On the physical level, success is often seen as specific material accomplishments—a particular type of car, home, status, or income level. However, once the car, home or other material possessions are obtained, there is no further growth in understanding, wisdom, or consciousness. Those who operate on this material level of success generally become consumed with maintaining those possessions that represent their success.

When success is understood on a spiritual level, it is seen as a progressive realization of a worthwhile purpose. You continue to grow and develop in all aspects. On a spiritual level, success is the continuous unfolding of your purpose and destiny.

True success is the progressive, continuous effort of attaining your goals and realizing your vision. This guides you to your worthwhile purpose in life.

Success Must Be In Your Mind First

Success starts in your own mind. Constantly have a concept and vision in your mind of what success means to you.

"You become what you think about most of the time."
—Earl Nightingale

Be Constant In Your Efforts

Never take a break from your success journey. Do not stop for rest and reward too soon. When you stop at the first sign of success, you become stagnant, lazy, and begin to decline. As your efforts begin to produce rewards and results, work even harder. Success and achievement come only through continuous work. The only place that success comes before work is in the dictionary.

Get Away From The Crowd At The Bottom

One of the most difficult steps you will face on your success journey is getting away from the crowd at the bottom. There are many unsuccessful, mediocre people who have failed to recognize, or act on their true potential. If you constantly associate with them, your success journey will be short-lived. You must clear the deck to make room for new associations which will complement and enhance your success efforts.

Once you break away from the mediocre crowd, accept the temporary state of loneliness and prepare for your success.

Be Willing To Change Your Life Completely

You must be willing to change your life completely. Make your life congruent with, consistent with, and harmonic with your desired success. Is there anything about the way you think or feel about yourself that will frustrate your success efforts? If so, handle it immediately. Do whatever it takes, for as long as it takes, to become the person that you must be, to accomplish your goals and realize your vision.

Every day, in every way
I'm getting better and better

Nine Rules For Becoming A Success

1. Do not procrastinate.

Do not wait until all conditions are right to become a success. You could wait the rest of your life. Believe that you always possess the understanding, courage and self-confidence to take action. Realize that procrastination is a state of mind.

2. Do it now.

Take the first step. There is always something you can do RIGHT NOW to move closer to your success. Use need, desire, ambition and attitude to motivate yourself to immediate action. Overcome thoughts of helplessness, limitation, lack, negativity, and failure.

3. Stand on your own two feet.

Do not depend on anyone or anything for your success. They may be depending on you. Believe that you already have everything you need to get everything you want. You should become independent as a part of your interdependence.

4. Do not fear failure.

To fail proves that you are trying. Every failure is a dress rehearsal for success. Every opportunity for success also contains the possibility for failure. Learn from your mistakes and failures. Concentrate on your possibilities for success.

5. Do not sell yourself cheaply.

You are worth exactly what you say you are worth. Know your full potential and the true value of your talents. Recognize that you are a very special individual with boundless capacity for health, wealth, happiness, love, success, prosperity and money.

6. Develop the success habit of being goal oriented.

Set realistic goals for yourself. Determine what must

be done to attain your goals. Make plans for their attainment. Keep a record of your performance and achievements. Stick to your goals until they are accomplished.

7. Visualize your goals and believe you can attain them.

See each goal clearly and in great detail in your mind's eye—your imagination. Develop a sensory relationship with your goal. Know how it looks, feels, smells, tastes, and sounds. See yourself as though you had already attained your goal. Hold that vision constantly in your mind and believe that you can and will accomplish it. Know that your goal will be achieved in a timely manner.

8. Plan your work, and work your plan.

Analyze your goal. Write down each and every action that must be performed to accomplish your goal. Make a plan for its attainment. Prepare a time schedule for the performance of each action. Execute your plan in accordance with your timetable and produce desired results. When you execute your plan effectively, you attract the attention of other people who will help you in your efforts.

9. Do not quit.

To quit demonstrates your own lack of belief in yourself. *Winners never quit, and quitters never win.*

When you get to the end of your rope,
tie a knot and hang on.
Be prepared to do whatever it takes,
for as long as it takes.

Levels Of Consciousness

On the most fundamental level, success is a matter of consciousness. There are three levels of mind or consciousness. They are: the **conscious mind,** the **subconscious mind,** and the **superconscious mind.** Each level of mind has its own characteristics.

The Conscious Mind

Your conscious mind is what you think. This is your rational, logical mind. It is masculine in nature and operates personally, selectively and judgmentally.

Your conscious mind creates and develops your thoughts. Your thoughts have two aspects: the idea— the statement of the thought—and the feelings associated with the thought. Your conscious mind transmits your thoughts to your subconscious mind through the feeling aspect of the thought.

The conscious mind reasons inductively. It proceeds to conclusions based on observation, experience, and education.

The conscious mind represents the world of effect.

The Subconscious Mind

Your subconscious mind represents what you are. It is your emotional, feeling mind. This subconscious mind is feminine in nature and operates impersonally, non-selectively, and non-judgmentally. It is non-selective in that in receives all ideas and gives them form and expression through feeling. It is non-judgmental in that it is not influenced by the truth or falsity of the ideas it receives. Your subconscious mind accepts every idea as true, and gives it form and expression through feeling.

It responds to persuasion, suggestion, and auto-suggestion. The subconscious mind reasons deductively. It proceeds on the assumption of truth of every idea, and develops a system of logic which will objectify (manifest) that truth in accord with the feelings associated with it.

The subconscious mind represents the world of cause.

The Superconscious Mind

The superconscious mind is the source of all creativity and faith. It is your spiritual mind, which is neither masculine nor feminine. Your superconscious mind operates on a subconscious level at all times. It has complete and total access to all ideas, feelings, and information stored in your subconscious mind. It also has unlimited access to all knowledge and information in existence.

Your superconscious mind is the source of all intuition, inspiration and internal motivation. It is capable of goal-oriented motivation, and is stimulated by clarity of thought and decisiveness of actions. The superconscious mind responds to clear authoritative commands by releasing ideas and energy.

Your superconscious mind is independent of time. The past, the present, and the future are one and the same. It is identified with the God Mind.

Procedurally, you have a thought in your conscious mind. The feeling aspect of this thought stimulates the subconscious mind, which communicates and interacts with the superconscious mind to objectify, or manifest the thought in your life experience.

Harmonic Relationships

The basic principle of the universe is that of order. When order is extended over a time period, it becomes harmony. This universal harmony is like a great symphony in which all notes, vibrations, and sounds are being played at the same time, for all time.

Each entity, each person, each life form is a note, a vibration in that great universal sound. When your life is in order, your goals are attained and your visions are realized. Your purpose is fulfilled, and you are in a complete harmonic relationship with the universe. The note and vibration that is your life is in perfect harmony with the universe. When this perfect harmony is achieved, you become one with the universe, and, upon death, leave your physical body at the proper level of consciousness to ascend to the next level of universal existence.

When your life is out of order, your goals are not being attained, nor is your vision realized. You are not in a complete harmonic relationship with the universe.

How do you know that your life is out of order?

You feel it. You are not happy. You are not clear about where you are going. You fear the future, and suffer anxiety, stress and a host of other unpleasant feelings.

How do you get your life in order?

You study the universal principles of the universe, and then align yourself with these principles. The extent to which you align yourself with these universal principles determines the extent to which your harmonic relationship with the universe can move toward completion. The way that you align yourself with the principles is to study, implement and master them. The better you get, the more complete your harmonic relationship with the universe. Once you are *on the path*, it is an endless cycle of growth, illumination and elevation to the next level to be mastered.

The following chapters lay out the laws of success and demonstrate their universal application. These principles will aid and assist you as you move toward the completion of your own harmonic relationship with the universe.

Seven Basic Harmonic Relationships.

1. The first harmonic relationship is the relationship between you and God—the generic Universal Intelligence, Consciousness, Force, and Source that is common to all religions and cultures. **Self with Source.**

2. The second harmonic relationship is the relationship between you and yourself. **Self with Self.**

3. The third harmonic relationship is the relationship between you and other people. **Self with Others.**

4. The fourth harmonic relationship is the relationship between you and your powers. **Self with Energy.**

5. The fifth harmonic relationship is the relationship between you and your objectives. **Self with Objectives.**

6. The sixth harmonic relationship is the relationship between you and that which you achieve. **Self with Results.**

7. The seventh harmonic relationship is the relationship between you and your life purpose. **Self with Purpose.**

Use of the Bible

References will be made to various biblical passages throughout this book. The Bible is used as a source of spiritual principle and as a textbook in universal law. It is used because this author is more familiar with the Bible than with other religious or spiritual texts. If each of the spiritual texts from all the various religions were studied, the same basic principles would be found.

In quoting from the Bible, I have taken the literary license to change the gender from the masculine *he*, or the feminine *she*, to the universal gender, *they* or *we*.

Throughout this book we will be studying the process through which thoughts are transformed into results.

The Process By Which Thoughts Become Things (Results)

Thoughts

Feelings

Vision

Goals

Plans

Actions

Results

Your thoughts manifest in accord with your feelings about those thoughts. You then create a vision, and reduce that vision to specific goals; then make plans to achieve those goals; take action in accord with your plans; and results appear. If any step along this process is missed, or not effective, it is reflected in the results obtained. Results are always obtained. Whether these are the results you desired, depends on how effectively you followed this process.

The Stages of Life

The key to a successful life is to realize that living is a learned habit, an acquired skill.

This learning begins at conception and continues through death. In the course of learning these lessons in living, your level of consciousness develops and grows. You begin to have certain realizations and understandings of what you must know to live a successful and happy life.

The first realization of life is that life is a garden, and you are the gardener.

Your garden can be well tended, neatly groomed and contain some of the most beautiful flowers—positive attributes or experiences. Or, it could be overrun by weeds—negative thoughts and emotions—until the flowers are no more.

The second realization of life is that every action, including inaction, has a definite result.

"Whatsoever a (mind) soweth,
that shall (they) also reap."
—Galatians 6:7

Soweth nothing, Getteth Nothing.

In a garden, if you do nothing, things do not remain status quo. Weeds will grow on their own. In life, if you do not affirmatively cultivate your flowers—your talents and gifts from the Creator, your life will be overrun with weeds—negative thoughts, emotions, and experiences. If you do not change, and take action to remove the weeds from your life, your talents will be consumed and taken away.

The third realization of life is that all things have a season.

Life has seasons or stages. These stages, though somewhat chronological, are based on your thoughts, attitudes, emotions, and associations at particular periods in life. Each stage lasts from 20 to 25 years. There are certain things that you must come to terms with and master in each stage of life. Anything you do not master at any particular stage will linger on as a potential challenge in subsequent stages.

The fourth realization of life is that there are only two forces at work in the universe—the forces of good and the forces of evil.

The universe is harmonic. All things that take place are either operating on behalf of good or evil. As you use your power to make things happen, the things you make happen are either on behalf of good, or on behalf of evil.

The Four Stages Of Life

Education
Sensation & Experience
Power
Immortality

The First Stage of Life is the stage of education.

This stage generally lasts from conception to 20 or 25 years of age. During this stage you learn the basic fundamental rules of the game of life. You formulate or accept a value system. You get your basic instruction in reading, writing, counting, logic, and decision making. Generally, in the education stage, you lay the foundation—thoughts, attitudes, emotions, and associations—on which the rest of your life is based.

It is in this first stage that you develop your basic attitude towards yourself—your self image. You also develop your attitude toward other people, and toward the world in general. It is here that you develop self-confidence or fear; faith or doubt; cowardice or courage. Your nature—positive or negative, thief or benefactor—is molded.

The challenge in this first stage is that most of your education comes from other people. You, as a child or young adult, had very little input in the matter. Thus, the thoughts, attitudes, emotions, and experiences, positive or negative, of your parents, teachers, ministers, or any other authority or admiration figure, tend to be perpetuated in the child and young adult.

If this foundation stage is not laid down solidly, then very often, at some point later in life, that crack in the foundation will manifest. It will show up like a thief in the night and snatch away your peace of mind, your good health, your glory, and your possessions.

When this foundation is built on truth, honesty, love, faith, discipline, confidence, compassion, and all of the positive aspects and attributes, then nothing is impossible. The young adult who has properly completed this stage of education is now properly prepared for the next three stages, and the rest of their lives.

Learn — Practice — Master

The Second Stage of Life is the stage of emotion, sensation and experience.

Chronologically, the second stage ranges from 20 or 25 years to 40 or 50 years of age. This is the stage where you begin to experiment and find out things for yourself. It is in this second stage that you truly experience the living process. You generally strike out on your own and face the challenges of an adult reality. Here you experience love, sex, alcohol, drugs, competition, insecurity, success and failure, frustration, and all the other sensations which make life exciting, intense, and challenging.

It is in this second stage that many people get stuck for

a major portion of their lives. As the stark realities of life confront them at every turn, they can get hooked on a feeling, a sensation, a person, a drug, or other addiction. They use their addiction as a means to escape or cope with their life situation.

It is in the second stage when your habits tend to make you or break you. Here you must develop and master the art of self-discipline. You must learn to control your thoughts, emotions, and appetites. It is in this second stage that you are challenged by the realities of survival. What does it take to keep a roof over your head and food on the table for you and your family, and still have time, energy, and resources for continual personal growth and development?

Some people get stuck on the treadmill of day-to-day survival, where appetites and crises constantly confront them from the cradle to the grave. To properly move through this second stage, you must master the skill of survival.

Mastering the skill of survival requires that you develop and implement a financial program in which your income exceeds your expenses. All of your financial dealings should be in accord with a realistic pre-established budget. You must develop discipline in overcoming the urge for immediate consumption or gratification. Systematically, set aside a portion of your income for wealth building. Take advantage of the benefits of investing and compound interest to establish a body of wealth for your personal peace of mind and enjoyment. Use a portion of your wealth to help fund and provide capital for your children and their future. Invest in worthwhile projects.

Men have a tendency to get stuck on the feelings generated by sex, alcohol, power, and physical conquests.

Women get stuck in the search for love or attention. The essence of the second stage of life is the search for a particular feeling. The challenges of this stage are centered on self-discipline and personal mastery of your physical and emotional appetites.

The Third Stage of Life is the stage of power.

It is in this stage that you perfect your ability to make things happen. This stage ranges from 40 or 50 years to 60 or 75 years of age. It should all come together in this third stage of life. During this stage, you generally attain your greatest successes and experience your greatest failures.

Having learned the basics of life and mastered your appetites and emotions, it is during this third stage that you learn how to reach down to the very core of your being and pull out just a little bit more of whatever is needed. Here, you master the laws of success and help others do the same. You master the skill of multiplying your powers through the efforts of others.

The challenge of this third stage of life is:

". . . chose you this day whom you will serve . . ."
—Joshua 24:15

You either serve good or evil. It's your choice.

The third stage is where your true mettle comes out. It is also where you are forced to repeat lessons that you should have mastered in previous stages, but did not. The challenges that confront you, and how you handle them, bring about a reality adjustment as to who you really are inside. It is in this stage that you establish or accept the type of human being that you would like to be.

The Fourth Stage of Life is the stage of immortality.

Only when you have fully mastered the power stage will you be able to effectively move into the stage of immortality. This fourth stage is generally from 60 or 75 years to 75 or 100 years of age. In this stage, you assess what you wanted to accomplish in your life—your purpose.

Evaluate the donations or contributions you have to give to the world. What can you give, or how can you live so that those contributions outlive your existence? It is at this point in your evolution that you must become a visionary, and see things as they can be, rather than as they appear to be. Create in yourself something that extends beyond the boundaries of one lifetime.

Reach within and summon the forces and vibrations, that you can initiate and direct in the present. Cultivate those strong forces and vibrations to create a presence that will continue to grow beyond your lifetime.

Your vision of immortality cannot be centered on the self, personal desires, or ego. Center it on the positive aspects of service and benefit to humanity. You must address a positive, worthwhile need in the world.

In this fourth stage of life, you may become obsessed with realizing your vision for immortality. This obsession is created by a deep desire to manifest your vision, fueled by total faith in the Creator and in your own abilities. The dynamic of obsession stimulates your mental, physical, spiritual, and psychic powers to an ultimate level. Consequently, you become magnetic, attracting the people and resources needed to realize your vision. You will be invincible. You will not be stopped or defeated, no matter what obstacles appear in your wake.

The time periods given for each stage are average for most people.

However, there are certain people to whom the time periods may not accurately apply. Many truly great figures in history had relatively short lifespans. A close inspection of their lives reveals that they probably experienced the four stages, but at a greatly accelerated pace.

Joan of Arc achieved immortality by the time she was burned at the stake when she was 19 years old. Alexander the Great, by age 32, achieved immortality through conquering most of the then-known world. Martin Luther King touched the conscience of humanity and achieved immortality before he was 40 years old.

There are four types of people in the world.

1. The Players
2. The Watchers
3. The Wonderers
4. The Wanderers

If life were a game of baseball, **the Players** would be the people or teams on the field. These are the ones who have sacrificed and practiced until they are the best that they can be. They generally do what they love and love what they do. They reap the rewards of their efforts. The players use their powers to make things happen. They reach within to that well of power that they have developed to get the desired results. The Players take the risks and get the rewards.

Need a grand slam — Got a grand slam.

The Watchers are the spectators sitting in the stands watching others play the game of life. Watching somebody else get the money, the recognition, and the girl. Everyone who is not on the playing field is a spectator.

True Watchers are the people who never really try hard at anything. They may dream of being a Player. But at the first signs of difficulty, challenge, or disappointment, they discard their dreams and scurry off the playing field of life, silently vowing never to try that again. These wannabe Players take their seat in the stands with carefully crafted excuses and explanations for not being in the game. Watchers are generally people who had a dream, but let it be compromised. Watchers often say, *"I should have done this, or I could have been that, but I've had a good life."*

The Wonderers are the people in the parking lot outside the stadium where the game of life is being played. They hear the sounds of the players and the spectators, but they are not a part of the game. They know something is going on, but they must wonder what it is, since they can't see. Wonderers learn about what's going on secondhand. They live their lives responding to outside stimuli, and developing other peoples' programs. They often see the world in terms of would have, could have, and should have.

The Wanderers are the people who are lost on the dirt road to the freeway, to the parking lot, outside the game of life. They have no idea of what is going on, and no plans to find out. The Wanderers are like thistles in the wind. They blow from pillar to post, without goals, plans, or roots. Ruled by their addictions and their appetites, they live for the moment and nothing more.

Chapter Summary

As you undertake the path of personal mastery, you must develop and perfect your study skills. The SQ3R Study Method is an effective tool to improve your learning and retention skills. Understanding the concepts and terminology of success prepares you for your success journey. Applying the nine rules for becoming a success, greatly enhances your prospects for desired results.

The concepts of the conscious, subconscious, and superconscious minds are key elements of the personal growth process. The fundamental principles of the universe, order and harmony, are expressed in the seven basic harmonic relationships. The process by which thoughts become things (results) shows how to obtain desired results in your life.

Successful living is a learned skill. Life is a garden and you are the gardener. Every action has consequences. Life has four seasons or stages. Each stage has a time period and is characterized by your thoughts, attitudes, emotions, and associations. There are certain lessons that must be mastered in each stage. Anything not mastered is a potential challenge in subsequent stages.

There are four basic personality types that most people fall into. Since you may become whatever you want to be, the choice is up to you.

Study Guide

1. In the SQ3R Study Method, what does the S stand for? The Q?, R(1)?, R(2)?, or R(3)?

2. Which of the "Nine Rules For Becoming A Success" do you need to work on first?

3. What will you do to improve in that area?

4. Of the seven steps by which thoughts become things, which ones should you concentrate?

5. In which stage of life are you right now? Why?

6. What must you do to move to the next stage?

7. Of the four types of people in the world, which type are you?

Chapter I

The Law
Of
Thought

The First Universal Law of Success is the Universal Law of Thought and Manifestation.

Thoughts become things (results) in accord with the nature and feeling of the thought. More personally, your thoughts manifest in your life experience, in accord with the emotions and feelings you associate with your thoughts.

One of the simplest statements of the Universal Law of Thought is:

> *"For as (they) thinketh in (their) heart,*
> *so (are they.) "*
> —Proverbs 23:7

To "think in their heart" means how they really feel

inside about those particular thoughts—which emotions and feelings are associated with them. A further illumination of *"in their heart"* is given in Matthew 6:21:

> *"For where your treasure is,*
> *there will your heart be also."*

Your *heart* is the center of your true feelings and emotions. It is always focused on the things that are important to you, your value system, and how you feel about yourself. For example, if you have the thought that financial independence is one of your primary objectives in life, then financial independence should begin to manifest in your life over a reasonable period of time. If it does not, then look into your inner feelings. Inside you may feel, for whatever reasons, that you are not worthy of financial independence. If you do not feel, in your heart— in your basic feeling nature about yourself— that you deserve the things, conditions, or circumstances that you describe in your thoughts, then they will not happen for you. They will not manifest in your life experience.

The essence of the Universal Law of Thought and Manifestation is that a thought has two basic aspects:

1. **A rational aspect**—the statement of the thought itself, the idea, the words.

2. **An emotional aspect**—the personal feelings and emotions associated with the thought.

> *"What you recognize* (in your thinking), *you energize* (in your feelings and emotions).
> *What you energize* (in your feelings and emotions), *you realize* (in your life experience)."
> —Rev. Ike

Three primary areas are covered by the Universal Law of Thought and Manifestation:

1. Thoughts you have about yourself—*your self-image*.
2. Thoughts you have about others—*your attitude*.
3. Thoughts you have about the world in general, your world perspective—*your outlook on life, your frame of reference*.

In this section, we will deal with the self-image only. The other areas, attitude and outlook, will be dealt with under the chapter on the Universal Law of Human Magetism.

SELF-IMAGE

How you see yourself in your own eyes determines what you get out of life. Self-image is your own conception of yourself. It is the mental and emotional picture you hold in your own consciousness of who you are, what you are, and what you represent.

Your self-image is important because it is the starting point of your life experiences. The image you hold of yourself is like a great vase into which all your life experiences are poured and blended.

If your self-image is a small, limited conception of yourself, based on ignorance, fear, doubt, and insecurity, then all of your experiences will be filtered through these same negative emotions.

On the other hand, if your self-image is based on knowledge, love, courage, respect, faith, and confidence, your life experiences will be filtered through these same positive emotions.

Self-image determines your capacity to give, receive, and interact with the life experiences and possibilities that confront you. Your self-image is like a magnet, attracting or repelling like or unlike qualities into your life experience.

You attract thoughts, people, and experiences which are congruent with how you think and feel about yourself. If you want to attract the good health, wealth and happiness that you desire and dream about, then you must develop a self-image that is compatible with and supports these very thoughts, namely good health, wealth, and happiness.

A nice example of how the self-image works is this:

One question that appears on just about every job application is: What salary and benefits are you expecting to receive? Many prospective employers give a lot of weight to how this question is answered. Subconsciously, most people will answer with a figure that indicates their own assessment of what they bring to the position.

A figure below what the position is worth is often a tip-off that the applicant has a low assessment of their own skills and would probably not be a good employee.

A figure too high above what the position is worth might indicate a lack of knowledge about the position itself. If you've done your homework and *know the deal*, you should be able to set a figure at the high end of what the position is worth, plus just enough fluff to get some attention. However, let me warn you. Be prepared to answer the question that will surely come - *"Why do you feel that you would be worth 2 zillion dollars to this company?"*

Have a well researched, well thought-out, well

presented, logical, and intelligent reply. You will probably get the position on your terms, consistent with your self-image.

Things Which Affect Your Self-Image

The most important aspects of the self-image are generally developed in the first stage of life. Once this self-image is fully established, all subsequent stages are built on and filtered through it. In fact, all changes in life begin with your self-image, and take place through changes in the feelings, emotions, and attitudes that it represents.

The three main things that effect your self-image are:

1. Thoughts, emotions, and feelings developed in the education stage of your life, particularly your early childhood—conception through age 7.
2. Environment.
3. Associations.

Thoughts, Emotions, and Feelings

In the first seven years of life, children develop the basic system of values that will take them through life. It is during this period that the child learns and develops emotions and feelings of fear and reward, pain and pleasure, love and lack of love, guilt, blame and shame, praise and discouragement, curiosity or lack of interest, persistence or discouragement, respect or disdain, manners or crudeness, courtesy or callousness, and other positive or negative emotions and feelings.

Young children are sponges for thoughts, emotions and feelings. They thrive and blossom on good teaching, good thoughts, good feelings and positive emotions. Yet, they have no defense against bad teaching, bad thoughts, negative feelings, and negative emotions. At this young age, a child's ability to discern and discriminate the good from the negative has not yet fully developed. Whatever thoughts, teachings or experiences that young children are exposed to, go straight into their subconscious and conscious minds. They make a permanent impact upon a child's emotional and feeling nature.

This is the crucible in which a child's personal value system is molded. Unfortunately, a young child has virtually no defense or options in this education experience. But, it is on this emotional and feeling foundation that the rest of your life is built. Give thanks if it was a good and positive foundation. Get busy if it wasn't.

"Train up a child in the way he should go, and when he is old, he will not depart from it."
—Proverbs 22:6

It is these feelings and emotions that become associated with your thoughts as your self-image develops. Unless they are changed in later years, these feelings and emotions, developed as a child, guide and, to a large extent, determine your life experiences.

Environment

Your environment is a strong influence upon your self-image because it is a source of validation and confirmation. Suppose you have a poor self-image, and you live and work in a run-down area, in a poorly maintained home, in an otherwise negative environment. What does that negative environment do other than confirm your negative self image?

When you are exposed to a particular environment, if you remain in it for a period of time, you take on some of the characteristics and properties of that environment. If your self-image contradicts and conflicts with the characteristics and properties of your environment, you are confronted with three choices:

1. Change the environment.
2. Change your self-image.
3. Leave the environment.

Associations

Association brings about assimilation. John Lavater, a noted Swiss theologian, beautifully captured this thought, saying:

> *"Frequent intercourse and intimate connection*
> *between two persons make them so alike, that*
> *not only their dispositions are molded*
> *like each other, but their faces and*
> *tones of voice contract a similarity."*

You should primarily associate only with those persons who possess the traits and characteristics that complement the positive aspects of your self-image. Such positive associations will greatly enhance your own development, and help confirm and establish the vision, emotions, and feelings you have about yourself.

Five Signals of a Poor Self-Image

In doing your own personal analysis of your self-image, there are certain keys or signals to look for:

1. Putting the blame on someone else.

By putting the blame for your own circumstances and situation on someone else, you avoid taking responsibility for what you have really done to yourself. If you do not take responsibility for your condition, you cannot change it, nor can you grow through it.

That which you cannot grow through,
you will go through again and again.

2. Running away from your problems.

When you are confronted with a problem or challenge, how do you respond? Generally, you can do one of four things: Flee It, Fight It, Forget It, or Face It. It is only when you face your problems and challenges and consider them projects to be completed, that you grow stronger in faith and self-confidence. As your faith and confidence grows, your ability to handle greater problems and challenges improves.

3. Criticizing other people constantly.

Why do you criticize other people constantly? Is your criticism constructive and motivated by true care, concern and desire to help? Or, is it based on envy, jealousy, and thoughts of inferiority? If your criticism is not positive—based on love, respect, and a sincere desire to help and improve another person—then it is not constructive criticism and it does harm not only to the other person, but also to your own self-image.

4. Waiting for someone else to solve your problems/challenges.

When you wait for someone else to solve your problems and challenges, you neutralize your own possibilities for learning and growing through experience. What keeps you from taking action when a problem or challenge presents itself? Is it fear of failure that you won't do the right things? Or is it fear of success that contradicts how you really feel about yourself? Whether it is the fear of failure or fear of success, it doesn't matter since the result is the same—procrastination, inaction, and ultimately, failure.

5. Pretending that everything is OK.

When you pretend that everything is alright, actively ignoring your problems and challenges, you subconsciously accept the consequences that will surely result from your inaction. You deceive yourself into thinking that there is no need for change or improvement, and develop a false sense of complacency. You eliminate virtually all possibility for personal growth and development. The nature of problems and challenges is that if they continue unresolved, they only get worse.

Problems vs. Projects

A first step in developing a self-image that works effectively in attaining your goals is to analyze your present and past experiences. Were you generally successful? Or did you give up and fail? How did you handle your successes and your failures? What did you do when confronted with serious problems? Do you continue going through the same problems again and again? Did you learn the lesson and move on?

Let's look at our terminology. The word *problem*, as generally understood, has a very negative connotation implying impassable objects, impossible people, adversity, and hardship. Calling something a *problem* creates tension, strain, and a fear that there may be no solution.

Using the term *project* to describe anything that you would normally call a *problem* suggests a positive endeavor of thoughts, feelings, and actions resulting in a particular desired outcome. In short, *problems* may or may not be solved, while *projects* are generally completed.

One has a far better attitude and frame of mind undertaking a project rather than solving a problem.

Using the word *challenge* instead of *problem* also gives a more positive spin to an impending confrontation. When you face a challenge, it creates a positive aura of calling together your troops and powers to meet a worthy opponent.

Can You Improve Your Self-Image?

Since so much of the self-image is developed during the first stage of life, particularly during those first seven years, is it possible during the second or even third stages to change the self-image to any significant degree? In fact, can you improve your self-image at all?

The answer lies in The Second Universal Law of Success. **If you can change your thinking on both the rational and emotional levels, then you can change the outcomes you experience in life.** We will address this more fully in the next chapter.

If you have a sincere desire and need to change your self-image, you can do it through deliberate, consistent, and effective practice of the twelve ways to improve your self-image.

How To Improve Your Self-Image

Imagine yourself to be a great artist, capable of creating a magnificent masterpiece. In addition to being the creator—the artist—you are also the work of art created—the masterpiece. You can recreate yourself through changing your self-image to that of the person you really want to be, having the things you want to have, and doing the things you want to do. However, I must warn you. It is not easy, and it may not be pretty. But neither is being a caterpillar—ugly, bound to the earth, and driven by hunger. Yet, if that caterpillar can survive a profound metamorphosis, it becomes a most beautiful butterfly, free to follow the wind and fly toward the sun.

You have the unique ability to create a new experience of life by changing your thinking about yourself. By constantly filling your mind with thoughts and feelings of the self-image you desire, you can—through persistent application—create that very self-image in your own life experience.

There are many ways to improve and develop your self-image. It can be developed into a powerful magnet, capable of attracting the right people, the right circumstances, good health, wealth, happiness, and anything else that you can see in your mind's eye, and feel in your heart. This process of growth from whom and what you are, to whom and what you want to become is called *the Work!*

Twelve Ways To Improve
Your Self-Image

1. Be honest with yourself.

Do not deceive yourself. Deceiving yourself is another way of pretending that everything is alright. When you are not honest with yourself, you totally defeat your quest for improvement and bury your potential self-image under layers of illusion and deception.

You are like the gardener who pretends that there are no weeds in the garden as he busies himself planting new flowers. One day he looks up from his planting and realizes that, in spite of all his efforts, the weeds have consumed his garden. When you are not honest with yourself, you destroy your possibilities for growth and improvement. And, the weeds will consume your garden.

2. Develop your imagination.

Your imagination is the blueprint for your future reality. It is the first step in the creative process.

"Where there is no vision, the people perish;
but (they) that keepeth the law, happy (are they.)"
—Proverbs 29:18

What is "the law" referred to in the scripture? It is the Universal Law of Thought and Manifestation.

If you can think it, you can do it.
If you can visualize it, you can become it.

Through your imagination, nothing is impossible. Develop your imagination by reading stimulating material. Get involved with exciting, successful people who can expand your realm of experience. Meditate daily and engage in artistic endeavors. See more possibilities in every experience and every relationship.

Once your vision—your thoughts about yourself and the world—is firmly grounded in your imagination, it cannot fail to be realized.

Where your imagination leads,
your reality will follow.

3. Be able to relax.

Relaxation is the key to stress reduction, and to mental and physical regeneration. Through relaxation you can communicate with your subconscious mind and tap into that well of universal knowledge, wisdom, energy, and understanding. Without the ability to regularly relax, you can, over time, become victim to accumulated stress. This accumulated stress can lower your energy level, impede your judgment, and actually cause physical illness. Simple tiredness can distract your efforts and change the outcomes you experience in your endeavors.

4. Have that winning feeling.

The winning feeling is a strong positive attitude of accomplishment. It is reflected in the way you walk, talk, and act. When you have that winning feeling, people notice it and are attracted to you. They become quite willing to aid and assist you on your path to accomplishment.

Everyone loves a winner.

5. Cultivate good habits.

Habits are actions or behavior patterns that become automatic over time, through frequent repetition and consistency. Good habits are those which induce positive cycles of good health, proper rest, a balanced diet, regular exercise, and right thinking. By developing good habits, you establish a harmonic relationship with all that's good for you.

*"Sow an act and you will reap a habit;
sow a habit and you reap a character;
sow a character and you will reap a destiny."*
—G. D. Boardman

*"The chains of habit are generally too small to be felt
until they are too strong to be broken."*
—Samuel Johnson

When you strip away all other excuses and explanations, where you are right now, whatever is going on in your life, positive or negative, is a direct result of your habits.

We make our habits, then our habits make us.

6. Aim to be happy.

Have a great sense of expectancy each day. Expect each day to be full of happiness. Experience each day from a perspective of happiness. Focus on the good and positive aspects of every moment. What you focus on, through faith, will happen. When you face each day with a great sense of anticipation and expectancy, you become magnetized for the object of your expectations.

Expect happiness and be happy.

7. Unmask.

A mask is a personality trait that you create and project to the world. Its purpose is to hide the real you. Masks are symbols of insecurity and self-doubt. They are often the result of someone else's expectations for you. When you wear a mask to create a facade to please someone else, it is generally at the expense of suppressing the real you.

Remove the mask of someone else's expectations and stop deceiving yourself. As long as the mask remains, you cannot get to the underlying circumstances that caused you to create it. Neither can you get to that part of yourself that you need to change to improve your self-image. The moment you remove the mask, you feel as though a great weight has been lifted. For the first time in a long time, you can see the person behind the mask and begin *the Work* of discovering the real you.

8. Have compassion.

You must be sensitive to the needs of others and be willing to give assistance. As you progress along your success journey, you can acquire a greater sensitivity and a greater responsibility to the plight and condition of others. This human sensitivity puts you in harmony with your Creator, and elevates the quality of your own being.

According to Genesis 1:28, we have dominion over every living thing on the earth. This godlike dominion implies that it is our duty to be sensitive to and respond to the needs of others. This does not just apply to human beings, but to all things which live upon the earth. So, you must have compassion for, and be sensitive to the plight and needs of all living things—people, animals, plants, and the environment.

9. Grow from your mistakes.

No one has ever succeeded without making mistakes. If you are making mistakes, at least you know that you are trying. *Mistakes are life-lessons in wisdom.*

Often, you learn more from your mistakes and failures than from your successes. You determine what works in a particular situation by learning what does not work and then trying again. One who has never made a mistake has probably never made a discovery.

Let your mistakes, through intelligent analysis and corrective actions, become markers showing the way on on your journey to improve your life.

Nothing beats failure like success.

10. Acknowledge your weaknesses.

Any weakness or personal shortcoming that is not acknowledged cannot be overcome. Refusing to acknowledge your weaknesses causes rationalization and deception, and therefore perpetuates that very condition.

11. Be Yourself.

People who pretend to be someone or something other than themselves never discover who they really are. When you try to be someone else, you become separated from your true self. As long as you are separated from your true self, your energies are diluted and your personal magnetism is greatly diminished. When you are true to yourself, you are in harmony with yourself, with other people, and with the world around you.

12. Never stop growing.

Life is a constant orchestration of growth through adversity and challenge.

The moment you reject the growth principle of life, you accept the static principle of death. The only way to attain the good health, wealth, happiness, and prosperity you seek and deserve is to grow into these qualities and attributes. To maintain them, you must continue to grow in knowledge, understanding, and consciousness.

Improving and developing your self-image into a positive, most effective tool, is the best first step you can take on building the new you. It is upon your newly developed self-image that the foundation for the mansion of your dreams is built. If this foundation is based on doubt, fear, and negativity, your mansion cannot stand. But, if it is built on truth, courage, compassion, self-confidence, and faith, your mansion stands on solid ground, and it will stand forever.

Chapter Summary

The Universal Law of Thought is the foundation of your life experiences. These experiences begin with your self-image, the thoughts you have about yourself. Your self-image is primarily influenced by your thoughts, emotions and feelings; your environment; and your associations. It may either be positive or negative.

A positive self-image is based on knowledge, love, courage, respect, faith, and confidence. A negative, or poor self-image, is based on ignorance, fear, doubt, and insecurity. The five signals of a poor self-image give specific character traits found in those with a poor self-image. The twelve ways to improve your self-image provide simple, easy to follow instructions for change and personal growth.

Study Guide

1. Do any of the five signals of a poor self-image apply to you?

2. Which ones, and why?

3. How are you doing *the Work*?

4. Which of the twelve ways to improve your self-image should you focus on first?

Chapter II

The Law
Of
Change

The Second Universal Law of Success is the Universal Law of Change.

> *"And be not conformed to this world,*
> *but be ye transformed*
> *by the renewing of your mind . . ."*
> —Romans 12:2

"Be not conformed to this world . . ." means that you are not locked in to whatever circumstances, situations, associations, challenges and so on that exists in your life right now. You do not have to remain in your present condition.

"Be ye transformed by the renewing of your mind . . ." means that you can be changed or transformed from your

present condition by putting a new thought, a new state of consciousness, into your mind. In other words, *you can change your life from whatever it is right now (this world) to anything you want it to be, by changing your thinking, your frame of reference about yourself.*

Taking the first and second universal laws of success together, the first law says that your experience of life depends on your thinking. The second law provides that the life you are experiencing right now can be changed by changing your thinking.

Some people seem to be successful in whatever they do. It doesn't seem to matter which political party is in charge, or how the economy as a whole is doing. Because they keep their thinking centered on the positive aspects of the results they wish to accomplish, they get just those results, no matter what.

The Universal Law of Change Has Three Fundamental Aspects: Faith, Choice and Desire.

The first aspect of the Universal Law of Change is faith.

Faith is defined as a firm belief or trust in something or someone, generally for which there is no objective proof. It is a belief from which all doubt has been removed. The biblical definition of faith makes it very clear:

> *"Now faith is the substance of things hoped for,*
> *the evidence of things not seen."*
> —Hebrews 11:1

In order to bring about change in your life, you must have faith that such change is possible. No matter how negative your situation, how absolutely overwhelming it may appear to be, if you have faith that things will get better, that there is something better for you in this life, then you have taken the first step toward finding it.

If you have doubts that your life can change for the better, then you're right, it can't. You must know, believe and have total faith that you are the creation of the God Head (God Consciousness), endowed with certain inalienable rights to be healthy, happy, and totally fulfilled.

The second aspect of the Universal Law of Change is choice.

"Choose this day whom you will serve . . ."
—Joshua 24:15

Every opportunity, every challenge that we experience confronts us with a choice. We choose either a positive approach (flowers), or a negative approach (weeds). Even if we make no affirmative choice at all, an approach is selected by the *world mind* which, in this cycle, is generally negative.

In order for you to change your life for the better, you must affirmatively identify and specifically define what a better life means to you. And you must choose to pursue this better life you have defined for yourself, and make the changes in your thinking and acting that will bring it about. An example of this principle is described in the parable of the prodigal son (Luke 15: 11-32).

To loosely summarize the parable: the youngest son

of a rich man asked his father for his piece of the rock. His father gave him his share and the young man went out into the world and partied his fortune away. Once he was broke, times got very tough and he suffered and hungered. In final desperation, he finally got a job feeding someone else's pigs. Even though he had a job, he still suffered and hungered to the point that he was seriously thinking of eating whatever the hogs didn't want. He had hit rock bottom with no plan to escape, and no one would bail him out or help him.

But then in verse 17, it states: *"And when he came to himself, he said, 'How many of my father's hired servants have bread enough and to spare, and I perish with hunger!'"*

The prodigal son renewed his mind, thought a new thought about himself. Though he was in the pigpen of life, suffering and hungry, he was still the son of a rich father.

Then he made his choice: He chose to serve his father (positive) rather than serve the owner of the pig pen (negative).

Verse 18 states: *"I will arise and go to my father . . ."* and beg for a job doing anything.

He then took action pursuing his choice. Verse 20: *"And he arose, and came to his father . . ."* He begged for a job, but his father wouldn't hear it. His father treated the prodigal son like who he really was, a long lost son of a powerful father, not a servant. Because the prodigal son had chosen to return home and serve his father, his father joyfully received him. His son, *"who was dead, . . . is now alive again."* Had the prodigal son made another choice, he would have gotten a different result.

The third aspect of the Universal Law of Change is desire.

The key ingredient for change is desire—burning desire. Unless there is a deep hunger, a burning desire for the changes you want to bring about in your life, these changes will not happen.

Once upon a time, in a place not far away, a diligent student questioned his master teacher on the meaning of deep desire. The teacher took the eager student down to the ocean and walked out into the water until it was nearly chest high. He then took the student and held his head under water for almost a minute. As the student began to struggle, craving for air, the teacher continued to hold him firmly under the water until the young student's body became limp. Then, within seconds of drowning the student, the teacher pulled his head out of the water as he gasped for a life saving breath of air.

The teacher then said, "You must desire the change in your life as strongly as you wanted to take that first breath. That is deep desire."

If your life is not the way you want it to be, then *know that you can do better.* Choose a positive, empowering approach to doing better. Desire this change in your life so badly that nothing and no one can stop you from achieving it. And, it will happen. You will have the better life you are seeking.

If it's that easy, why are there not more successful people in the world? What is it that keeps people from making the changes in their life that they know must be made in order to become the person they would like to be, and experience the better life they are seeking?

"You can be what you want to be.
Do what you want to do.
Have what you want to have."

—Rev. Ike

Obstacles To Change

The main obstacle to change is fear.

What is fear?
(F) False (E) Evidence (A) Appearing (R) Real.

Three main fears keep people from making the changes that are necessary to improve their lives:

1. The fear of change.
2. The fear of criticism.
3. The fear of failure.

Some people fear change itself. They may say they want to change certain aspects of their life, but at the same time, they're doing everything possible to keep their situation exactly the way it is right then.

This fear of change sometimes manifests as a fear of the unknown. One of the pitfalls of being successful but unfulfilled is that it is easy to become complacent and satisfied with what you have accomplished. When this happens, you become fearful of making changes because you're not sure how it's all going to work out.

You overcome the fear of change by having total faith that you can realize the outcomes desired in your new life. Know that your father, the God Head, is rich and powerful, and eager to bestow all good things unto you.

The fear of criticism robs you of your initiative and destroys your imagination. It is fatal to your personal achievement, and encourages the development of inferiority complexes. When you fear the criticism of others, your desire for change is neutralized, and you remain stuck in the very condition you want to change.

To overcome the fear of criticism, you must realize that all criticism is not harmful. Consider the source of the criticism. Is it coming from someone who has already accomplished what you are trying to do, or who is otherwise successful and fulfilled in their own endeavors? Or is the criticism coming from someone who is unsuccessful in whatever they attempt? Is the criticism motivated by true care and concern, or is it motivated by jealousy and feelings of inferiority?

When criticism is constructive and comes from someone you respect, pay attention to what they are saying, and intelligently analyze their statements. Make the required adjustments and continue making the changes desired in your life.

If the criticism comes from someone you do not respect, tune them out and continue with your program.

If you search throughout recorded history, you will never find a statue erected to a critic. Statues are erected for the doers, those who take on the challenge of change victoriously, and go on to do great things in the world.

Overcome the fear of criticism by refusing to worry about what other people think, say, or do. When people criticize you, it's a good bet that you're doing something right. Those who are qualified to give constructive criticism will find a way to do so which makes you feel empowered.

The fear of failure keeps you from trying. Fear of failure often manifests as the habit of procrastination. This way, you can talk about the better life you desire and know the changes in your thinking that are necessary to bring this better life about. Yet, you never seem to get started making those changes. It's either too late, too early, or just not the right time to get started. The fear of failure makes you find rational excuses for not trying, and understandable excuses for quitting—often just a step away from victory.

To overcome the fear of failure, realize that to fail means you're trying. Failure is just a dress rehearsal for success.

Anyone who has not failed at anything,
has probably never succeeded at anything either.

Your attitude toward failure determines your aptitude for success. An excellent example of one's attitude toward failure can be found in the life of Thomas Edison. Shortly before inventing the light bulb, Thomas Edison was being interviewed by a young reporter. The reporter asked Mr. Edison why hadn't he given up on this light bulb idea, since he had failed on over 3,000 attempts to make the light bulb work. Mr. Edison looked at the reporter and said "Failed? I have never failed. What I have done is successfully identify 3,000 ways that will not work."

Recognize that you can change your condition by changing your thinking: about yourself, about your condition, and about the people with whom you associate. The key to experiencing a better life lies is your ability to fully and completely describe the vision of the life you wish to experience, and of the person you would like to become.

Chapter Summary

The Universal Law of Change provides that the life you are experiencing right now can be changed by changing your thinking. However, in order to affect this change requires three things: you must have faith that there is something better for you; you must choose to do better; and you must truly desire to change.

Fear of change, fear of criticism, and fear of failure are the main obstacles to change. To overcome these obstacles, you must have total faith in God, in yourself, and in your abilities. Don't worry about what other people think, say, or do. Treat each failure as a dress rehearsal for success. Know that anyone who has never failed has probably never succeeded at anything, either.

Study Guide

1. How can you become the person you want to be?

2. What is the main obstacle keeping you from becoming that person?

3. How will you overcome that obstacle?

Chapter III

The Law
Of
Vision

The Third Universal Law of Success is the Universal Law of Vision.

"Where there is no vision, the people perish;
but (they) that keepeth the law, happy (are they.)"
—Proverbs 29:18

Where you have no vision of where you want to go with your life, you will be miserable and fail to achieve a better life. Your vision of the life you would like to experience must be crystal clear in your mind. See the vision in great detail. Internalize your vision through your senses. Know how it looks, feels, smells, sounds, and tastes. By fully expressing your vision through your senses—your feeling nature—you energize it and harmonize it with the universal force that makes it happen in your life experience.

The *"law"* referred to in the second line of this scripture, is the First Universal Law of Success, the Law of Thought and Manifestation.

What you recognize (your vision), **you energize** (through your feelings).

What you energize (through your feelings), **you realize** (in your life experience).

The Universal Law of Vision Has Two Aspects: Specificity and Imagination.

The first aspect of vision is specificity.

"And the Lord answered ...
Write the vision, and make it plain upon tablets
that (they) may run that readeth it.
For the vision is yet for an appointed time,
but at the end it shall speak, and not lie;
though it tarry, wait for it,
because it will surely come, it will not tarry."
—Habakkuk 2:2,3

You must be specific about your vision. Write it down clearly and in great detail, that you may execute your plan to realize it. Have faith and know with assurance that your vision will be realized at the proper time. It will surely happen, if you just do not quit.

The aspect of specificity is further expressed through your goals.

It is far easier to hit a target you can see
than to hit one you cannot see.

Goals

A goal is the line or place at which a race or trip is ended. Goals are the stepping-stones that guide you to your vision of who you are, what you are about, and whatever you want to achieve. You may make a goal of anything you wish to accomplish. Once you specifically define your vision of yourself—your better life—you should establish goals as the specific steps that will lead you to the realization of your vision.

Goals provide excellent opportunities to build your self-confidence. When you complete yourself with respect to a particular goal, by accomplishing it, you validate your own abilities and increase your self-confidence. As your self-confidence grows, so does your ability to successfully tackle more difficult goals.

Develop the habit of being goal-oriented. As your goals are accomplished, you grow and progress toward the vision of life you have for yourself. Where there are no goals to be systematically achieved, your vision of a better life cannot be realized.

Types of Goals

There are basically three types of goals: immediate, intermediate, and long range.

1. Immediate goals: *Goals that are closest, nearest, or next in order.* These goals represent tasks or objectives that may be accomplished quickly or without a great deal of effort and planning. Timewise, immediate goals may be accomplished in a day or so, or within a period of up to three months (1 to 90 days). There are three levels of immediate goals: Level I (1 to 30 days); Level II (30 to 60 days), and Level III (60 to 90 days).

2. Intermediate goals: *Midrange between immediate and long range goals.* Intermediate goals often require multiple steps and considerable planning for their completion. It usually takes the completion of a series of immediate goals to accomplish an intermediate goal. Intermediate goals require more consistent and continuous direction in your life. They may be completed in ninety days to two years. There are three levels of intermediate goals: Level IV (90 days to 6 months), Level V (6 months to 1 year), and Level VI
(1 to 3 years).

3. Long-range goals: *These goals take the future into consideration.* Often they are related to your life's work, career, and professional objectives. Long-range goals require extensive planning, preparation, and execution. They are consistent with and support your life vision or purpose. Your long-range goals are built on the consistent and continuous accomplishment of your immediate and intermediate goals. They may require from three years to a lifetime for their completion and accomplishment. There are three levels of long-range goals: Level VII (3 to 5 years), Level VIII (5 to 10 years), and Level IX (10 years to a lifetime).

Graphically the relationship between the three types of goals may look like this:

```
Immediate Goal #1 *
Immediate Goal #2 * * * Intermediate Goal #1 *
Immediate Goal #3 *
                            *** Long Range Goal #1
Immediate Goal #4 *                    *
Immediate Goal #5 * * * Intermediate Goal #2 *  *
Immediate Goal #6 *
```

The First Step

The first step toward realizing the vision you have for yourself is to write your vision down clearly and in great detail. Then, determine the steps that will lead you to your vision. Make these steps your goals. Write down each goal that must be accomplished, as concisely as possible, in the order of its importance and priority. Know what you want, your vision, and the specific steps which will lead you there. Your goals are giant steps towards realizing that vision.

Choosing Your Goals

Choose the goals that will lead you to your vision, in accord with your lifestyle, the things you are good at, and the things which you enjoy doing. Each goal should have certain important qualities that give you the best opportunity to accomplish it.

Six Qualities Every Goal Should Have

1. It should be written, committed to, and shared.

Writing your goals helps you crystallize exactly what you want to accomplish. Write each goal in one or two sentences. If it takes you an entire page to write your goal, chances are that you will not be able to attain it. A short, simple, concise goal statement is easier to think about, remember, and act on.

Once you have written your goal statement, read it

aloud at least three times per day. Think about it constantly. You must be committed to accomplishing each goal. Make a binding agreement with yourself that nothing and no one will stop you from attaining your goal. Give your time, efforts, expertise, resources, and anything else necessary to accomplish your goal.

Share your goal with someone special who understands and believes in what you are doing. Stay away from anyone who will discourage or criticize you. Very often, members of your own family and others close to you are the worst choices to tell about your goals. Be sure that the people with whom you share your goals will not be jealous or envious. They should have important goals of their own to accomplish, and be well on their way to accomplishing them. Remember that the purpose of sharing your goals is to establish accountability, and to obtain cooperation, assistance, and encouragement. Another perspective which offers knowledge, encouragement, and constructive criticism is also helpful.

2. It should be realistic and attainable.

One of the easiest ways to set yourself up for failure is to select improper goals. No goal is impossible, but it may be unrealistic at your particular state of development or at a given time. Make sure that your goals are realistic and attainable for you, based on where you are right now.

3. It should be flexible and reflect change.

Your goal is a statement and projection of your vision. However, as you begin to pursue your goal, external conditions and circumstances which are beyond your control may appear. Potentially, these things could prevent you from attaining your goal. When this interference occurs, do not become discouraged or abandon your goal. Make the necessary changes and modifications to your goal, or to the manner of pursuing it. That will neutralize the condition or circumstance that is blocking your way.

4. It should be concrete and measurable.

Your goal must be definite and specific. Clearly define it in terms of your senses: How does it look, feel, smell, taste, and sound. See your goal in terms of size, color, location, movement, and any other characteristic or property that can be perceived by the senses.

If your goal is not concrete and clearly defined, you will probably not be able to attain it. *Your goal is the outcome desired as a result of your organized efforts.* When the desired outcome—your goal—is unclear, then the energy and activities necessary to produce that outcome cannot be focused or directed effectively.

Your goal must be measurable to determine its dimensions. When a goal is measurable, you have a standard by which you can analyze it and estimate completion. If it is not measurable, it is extremely difficult to project when you will attain it, how far you have to go, or how much energy it will take. Having a goal that is not measurable is like going on a car trip to an undetermined destination. You ride and ride, but never get there.

5. It should be extended to cover certain time periods.

You must set a definite time period in which to

accomplish your goal. A definite time period gives you a standard by which to measure and regulate your performance.

Take special care in establishing a proper time for accomplishing your goal. This time period should be realistic in light of your particular level of skill, the time and resources you have available, time constraints of the goal itself, and benchmarks of past performance by yourself and others.

Putting a time component into your goal gives you a means by which to examine your performance and project your completion. If, based on monitoring your own performance, the projected time for completion is unreasonable or unacceptable, you can increase your efforts, modify your timetable, or even alter your goal accordingly.

6. It should be set in advance.

Your goal is a destination, the desired outcome of your endeavors. If it is not set in advance, then you cannot make plans, nor take effective steps to attain it.

When you set your goal in advance, you give a particular orientation to your life and bring focus to your energy and to your thoughts.

Categories of Goals

There are basically two categories of goals: *goals in continuity* and *goals in opposition*.

Goals in continuity are goals which are logical extensions of your present condition or situation, *enhanced by reasonable improvement.*

An example of goals in continuity would be: Upon graduation from high school, you decide to become a surgeon. The goals that will lead you to your vision of becoming a surgeon could be:

Goal #1 - get accepted to the college of your choice.
Goal #2 - graduate from college with a 3.8 grade
point average.
Goal #3 - get accepted to the medical school of your
choice.
Goal #4 - successfully complete medical school in
the top 5% of your class.
Goal #5 - get accepted to the hospital residency
program of your choice.
Goal #6 - successfully complete your medical
boards with high—top 5%— scores.
Goal #7 - secure a position with the best surgeon
at the hospital of your choice.

Each of these goals is a reasonable and logical extension of the prior goal.

Goals in opposition *are goals which represent a complete change in your current condition or situation.*

They may represent an abrupt change in the direction of your life. An example of a goal in opposition would be: after smoking a pack of cigarettes a day for the last twenty years, you decide today to quit smoking immediately.

Your stated goal, to quit smoking immediately, is a goal in opposition because it represents a complete change in what you have been doing for the last twenty years.

Goals in opposition are generally harder to accomplish than goals in continuity.

As you begin to develop your long-range goals, a bigger picture develops, one which encompasses these long-range goals and brings them together as the foundation of your purpose in life.

Purpose

Your purpose is what you want your life to represent. It is generally revealed through your long-range goals. Your purpose provides orientation and direction for your journey through life. It is your reason for living. Like a ship's compass, your purpose guides you when all else fails. No one can choose your purpose for you. Only you can determine it for yourself.

Your purpose is identified with the quality of your life. *It is not how long you live, but rather what you do.*

It is not the duration of your life, but the donation you make to life that really counts.

Many of the truly great achievers in history had relatively short lives.

You must be obsessed with your purpose. Eat it, sleep it, breathe it, think about it, and act on it every moment of every day.

Live your life so that the use of your life will outlive your life.

How To Develop Your Purpose

Ask yourself the following questions:

1. Am I the person I really want to be?
2. Am I living a meaningful life?
3. What am I doing to realize a meaningful life?
4. What am I doing to make my dreams and
   visions come true?
5. What important contribution do I have to
   make to the world?
6. What do I want my life to stand for?

When you answer these questions, be honest with yourself. Do not deceive yourself. Take your time and carefully analyze the questions and your answers. Once you can articulate the answers to these questions, immediately develop a plan of action to implement your answers.

Realize that in asking the above questions and implementing your answers, you are developing a pattern and rhythm for your life. The pattern for your life embraces the finite period of time from conception to death, but the rhythm of your life embraces all eternity.

The Rhythms of Life

The basic rhythms of life are the rhythms of peace, health, beauty, happiness, creative action, and abundance. When you superimpose your life-pattern onto these universal rhythms, you extend your essence and influence beyond the boundaries of your lifetime. You become one of those bigger-than-life figures that change the course of history, improve the condition of all mankind, and bring peace, truth, wisdom, and deeper understanding to the world.

Your life becomes a contribution to all humanity.

Establishing Your Purpose

A clearly defined purpose projects your life into eternity. Once you have identified your purpose, you can set a direction for your life. As you strive to realize your purpose, you harmonize with the rhythms of life which form your destiny.

Seven Guidelines for Establishing Your Purpose

1. It must be idealistic.

Always strive for the highest and best in all things. See things as they can or should be, rather than as they are. Use your imagination as a guide in establishing your purpose.

2. It must be visionary.

See beyond the horizon. Learn to perceive, remember, accept, and rely on your dreams. Do not be discouraged if your purpose appears to be impossible, impractical, or unrealistic to others. Visions are perceptions of higher states of consciousness. Visionary thought representations become the blueprints for your future reality. Your special mandate is to create reality from thoughts through vision.

3. It must be lifelong.

Your purpose in life rarely, if ever, changes. However, your perception of it may change, depending on your level of consciousness. Your purpose is your life's work, as you perceive it from moment to moment. It may extend well beyond the boundaries of your lifetime. In fact, the realization of your purpose may not occur until long after you have ceased to exist in physical form.

4. It must benefit everyone.

The continuous realization of your purpose goes far beyond the personal desires of your ego. A purpose centered on self, for the sole benefit of self, is no purpose at all. It is a personal goal. However, once your purpose goes beyond yourself and your ego, it will necessarily involve other people. This involvement must be positive and beneficial to all concerned.

5. It must be challenging.

Your purpose should make you stretch to reach your highest potential. It should be a continuous challenge to your faith and to your abilities. Your faith grows stronger as your efforts yield positive results. As your faith grows, so does your ability to face and prevail over even greater challenges.

6. It must set you on fire.

When your purpose sets you on fire, you become

obsessed with its immediate and continuous realization. Every moment of your life, you constantly think about it, talk about it, and act on it. The source of this fire from your purpose is your deep desire.

Deep desire causes you to exert every element of the power and energy you possess for the realization of your purpose. Deep desire and faith together create dynamic enthusiasm.

Dynamic enthusiasm is the burning fire which stimulates your mental, physical, and psychic powers to the point where they become infectious, contagious, and invincible.

7. It must be worthwhile.

Your purpose must fulfill a legitimate positive need in the world. A worthwhile purpose attracts the forces of the universe to aid and assist you in its continuous realization.

Once you identify and articulate your purpose, write it down. This is your statement to yourself and to the world of where you are going with your life. With this clear and concise statement of your purpose, you can determine what must be done for its realization. Then you can establish the goals which will guide you to your purpose, and make plans for attaining these goals.

Imagination

The second aspect of the law of vision is imagination. This is your power to form mental images of something not present to the senses. Albert Einstein once said,

"Imagination is more important than knowledge. For knowledge is limited, whereas imagination embraces the whole world, stimulating progress, giving birth to evolution."

Your imagination is the connecting link between your own human consciousness and the universal consciousness. Through your imagination, the formless energy of the universal mind becomes the formed universe in your own mind, and thus your life experience.

Your power of imagination is used to see beyond the appearances of your present situation, to the possibilities of who you really are and what you can become. As you do all you can to realize the vision you have of yourself, you must also appeal to your higher consciousness to raise your energy level. This requires that you bring yourself to a rested and peaceful (alpha) state, and create visual images in your mind of each and every aspect of your vision. Know that your mind is open and receptive to all beneficial ideas. Relax and let go, commanding the universal mind to reveal each and every good idea that will help implement your vision.

After a little practice, the ideas will begin to flow freely from the superconscious mind into your conscious mind. Learn to record these ideas in a systematic fashion and to implement them in your daily practice.

***Anything your mind can conceive
and believe, it can achieve.***

There are two types of imagination:

1. Synthetic Imagination.
2. Creative Imagination.

Synthetic Imagination

Through synthetic imagination, existing concepts, ideas, and plans are arranged into new combinations. This type of imagination operates through education and observation. A genius uses synthetic imagination to create something totally new.

Creative Imagination

Through creative imagination, your mind has direct communication and contact with Universal Intelligence. Creative imagination is the faculty through which hunches and inspiration come. It communicates through the subconscious minds of other people, and operates as a sixth sense. Though it operates automatically, creative intelligence is most productive when your conscious and subconscious minds are in harmony with it.

Your creative imagination can compensate for your lack of experience. It can help you out perform another person who has more experience, but a weak creative imagination.

How To Develop Your Creative Imagination

1. Stimulate your mind by reading.

Reading is the process through which great minds are developed. A *DAILY* reading program is a powerful tool that can expand the scope of your thoughts and enhance your powers of imagination. Read material which stimulates your thinking, challenges your personal belief system, and inspires you to right action.

2. Practice your imagination skills.

Imagination is a skill to be developed and mastered. Every form and shape originated in the imagination. It is through the imagination that the formless takes form. To most effectively develop your imagination skills, use the techniques of relaxation and meditation. On a daily basis, put yourself in a rest (alpha) state. Find a place to sit quietly. Close your eyes. Focus on your breathing and relax. Visualize familiar objects first. Progress to seeing your goals, thoughts, and ideas as visual images in your mind.

3. Have the goals you want to achieve and the purpose you want to realize clearly in your mind.

Develop mental images of the goals you wish to accomplish and a general idea of your life purpose. Write these goals in the shortest, simplest, most concise way. Your goals must be definite and specific. Describe each goal in the most sensory fashion, using as many of your senses as possible. How does it look, feel, smell, taste, and sound?

Analyze and organize your goals to help reveal your purpose. Read your goals aloud at least three times per day and contemplate your purpose.

4. Develop your powers of concentration.

Concentration is a learned skill. It is the process by which you focus your attention on a particular thought, thing, or outcome. Your powers of concentration come from your willpower and your self-discipline. Develop your powers of concentration by focusing your attention, your actions, and your feelings on your goals.

5. Always control your moods and emotions.

Moods and emotions are the vehicles used by the saboteur—the negative part of you—to create distractions, discouragement, distrust, doubt, indecision, and procrastination. This saboteur is neutralized by taking possession of your thoughts in such strength or degree that your emotions, your instincts, and your body are under your control. Remember, what you recognize, you energize. What you energize, you realize.

Creative imagination is enhanced by creative thinking. Creative thinking is finding new and better ways to do something. Success in any particular endeavor generally centers on finding ways to do things better.

Three Steps To Increase Your Creativity

1. Believe it can be done.

Before anything can be accomplished, you must first believe it can be done. This belief sets the mind in motion to find a way to do it. Whatever the mind believes is true. Believing something can be done paves the way for your creative imagination to find a way to do it.

2. Eliminate the word impossible from your vocabulary and from your thinking.

When you say or believe something is impossible, your mind sets out to prove why it cannot be done.

3. Always be receptive to new ideas.

Do not just hear new ideas, but listen to them intently. Analyze new ideas fully and completely, focusing on how and why they work, and how they may be a benefit to you.

How To Practice Your Creative Imagination Skills

1. Establish a specific time and place each day to practice creative imagination. This place should be conducive to thought and reflection.

2. Develop the habit of using your mind for new ideas.

3. Think in new, expanded dimensions beyond what you have been accustomed to thinking.

4. Participate in activities and exercises which expand you as a person.

5. Develop your emotions and instincts of wonder into a vivid imagination.

Four Ways To Develop Your Creativity

1. Realize that the creative genius does not come through your five senses, but rather through your "sixth sense," your subconscious mind.

2. Realize that your sixth sense can inspire, through your imagination, your five senses to dwell on (experience) an imagined reality (an inspired thought).

3. Realize that all your creativity comes from your subconscious mind.

4. Stand your ground and be positive. Your creative imagination can serve you as long as you are positive.

Chapter Summary

The Law of Vision requires that you have a crystal clear picture in your mind of what you want to be, do, and have. When this picture—your vision—is fully internalized through your senses, it begins to manifest in your life experience. By writing down your vision clearly and in great detail, you can analyze it, dissect it, and break it down into identifiable goals. Each goal has six qualities which facilitate its attainment.

As you review your long-range goals, your life purpose reveals itself. What do you want your life to stand for? What contribution will you make to the world? These are the questions that help guide you to your life purpose. The seven guidelines for establishing your purpose become your road map to immortality.

Your power of imagination is a critical tool in developing your creativity. It permits you to see beyond the appearances of your present reality to the possibilities of who and what you may become. Both your creativity and your imagination may be developed, refined, and expanded virtually without limitation.

Study Guide

1. Write your one-, two-, and five- year goals.

2. What is your purpose in life?

3. Which of the guidelines for establishing your purpose are most important to you?

Chapter IV

The Law
Of
Command

The Fourth Universal Law of Success is the Universal Law of Command. This universal law is stated at numerous places throughout the Bible.

> *"Thou shalt decree a thing*
> *and it shall be established unto thee . . ."*
> —Job 22:28

> *(a person) shall have*
> *whatsoever (they) saith."*
> —Mark 11:23

> *". . . command ye me."*
> —Isaiah 45:11

One of the most important keys to success is your ability to use the Universal Law of Command to get what you want in life. By applying this universal law, you can stimulate the universal cosmic forces that make desires and dreams manifest in reality.

The law of command is applied throughout the Bible. For example, according to the first chapter of Genesis, the world was spoken or commanded into existence,

> *"And God said, Let there be light:*
> *and there was light."*
> *"And God said, Let there be a firmament . . .*
> *and it was so."*
> *"And God said, Let the waters*
> *under the heaven . . . and it was so."*
> —Genesis 1:3,6,9

The Universal Law of Command is most often expressed as the Universal Law of Affirmation.

To affirm means to declare or state positively; to make a statement, confidently declaring it to be true. An affirmation is a statement in which you declare a desired outcome to be true, a fact. Applying the Universal Law of Command: thou shall decree a thing (your affirmation) and it (the desired outcome) shall be established unto thee (it will happen, manifest in your life).

For example, if you wish to eliminate financial challenges from your life, the first step is to change your thinking about your financial condition. This thought-renewing process can be started by affirming over and over, with feeling,

"I am financially secure!"

Affirming or commanding financial security as though you had already attained it conditions your thinking and stimulates your feelings. This sets the stage to manifest the very outcome you are affirming.

This manifestation of the outcome you desire does not come by haphazardly repeating your affirmation when you remember it, or feel like it. It is only through repeating your affirmation for a certain period of time—two or three times each day over a sufficient number of days—that you can internalize the affirmation in your feeling nature. Once the desired outcome stated in your affirmation is completely internalized in your feeling nature, it will manifest in your life.

Doubt is the main obstacle to successfully using affirmations to bring about changes in your life.

Do they work? Will they work for me? Jesus was very clear on the relationship between command or affirmation, and doubt, saying in Mark 11:23:

"For verily I say unto you,
Whosoever shall say unto this mountain,
Be thou removed,
and be thou cast into the sea;
and shall not doubt in (their) heart,
but shall believe that those things which
(they) saith shall come to pass,
(they) shall have whatever (they) saith."

If you consistently use an affirmation, and have total faith that you deserve, and are capable of attaining the desired outcome, then you shall have it.

The Universal Law of Command works positively or negatively.

If you affirm a negative outcome with feeling, you will get that too. Many experiences of failure and unhappiness can be traced to the operation of negative affirmations or negative commands. These negative affirmations are usually put into operation unconsciously by simple statements expressing negative outcomes.

For example, negative affirmations like *I can't do it, I know this won't work out for me,* or *I always catch cold when the weather changes,* become self-fulfilling prophecies. Negative affirmations tend to originate in your feeling nature, in how you feel about yourself. These negative feelings about yourself tend to subconsciously focus your thoughts on the negative outcomes expressed in the negative affirmation. These negative outcomes manifest in your life experience as failure, lack, limitation, and ill health.

The most devastating aspect of negative affirmations is that they are usually expressed on a subconscious level. Seemingly idle words and harmless statements, especially those which confirm negative feelings you have about yourself, can become negative affirmations established in your thoughts, and manifesting in your life. Isaiah 55:11 states:

"So shall my word be
that goeth forth out of my mouth;
it shall not return unto me void,
but it shall accomplish that which I please . . ."

Thus internalized negative affirmations, based on negative feelings about yourself, become stumbling blocks to your progress, and short circuit the manifestation of your vision—a better, more fulfilling life.

Twelve Affirmations To Live By

1. I have a positive self-image.
2. I believe in myself and my abilities.
3. I define my purpose and reason for living.
4. I think positively, with understanding and
faith that I can realize my purpose.
5. I constantly visualize my purpose, seeing it
clearly in my mind's eye.
6. I always focus on the positive.
7. I have the confidence and courage to be
inner directed.
8. I take possession of my mind in such strength
or degree that my emotions, my instincts, and
my body are under my control.
9. I always act in the present. I do it now.
10. I have a plan for my success.
11. I persist in my efforts with unshakable faith
in my own ability.
12. I execute my plan and produce desired results.

A Daily Affirmation Exercise

Write each affirmation on a 3X5 index card. Do this exercise when you get up each morning, and before you go to bed each night. Stand in front of your mirror, focus your eyes on your third eye. (Your third eye is a spiritual connection to the universal force. It is located slightly—an inch or so—above the imaginary line connecting your eyes, at the mid-point.)

Repeat each affirmation five times with feeling. Pick out one affirmation that you need to work on. Close your eyes and visualize exactly how your life would be if you already possessed the quality or attribute described in your affirmation.

Carry the index cards with you for the next twenty-one days. Pull them out and repeat your affirmations, with feeling, as often as possible during each day. When you read your affirmations over two or three times each day, be sure to add special emphasis and feeling to the specific affirmation you need to work on. The more consistently you use these affirmations—and any others you may create—with feeling, the quicker you will get the desired results.

Daily Affirmation

"Today is the most magnificent day of my life. Health, wealth, happiness, love, success, prosperity, and money come to me in great abundance."

Use this daily affirmation each morning to help you spring out of bed with a positive attitude and with positive expectations for the day.

Programming Your Life

Daily use of affirmations, with feeling, can start the process of change required to produce the person you want to be, and the outcomes you wish to experience.

"Today I go forth with a winning attitude."

"Today I go forth with a success attitude."

"Today I go forth with a money-making attitude."

Chapter Summary

The Universal Law of Command is one of your most effective tools for getting what you want in life. Using it stimulates the universal forces to be applied on your behalf. This universal law is most often expressed as the law of affirmation. To affirm means to make a statement in which you declare a desired outcome to be true. The Universal Law of Affirmation provides that whatever you affirm, consistently with strong feeling will, in fact happen. This universal law will either work for you—positively, or work against you—negatively. Using the law affirmatively, positive changes can be made in your life. Doubt neutralizes its effectiveness.

Study Guide

1. Which habits would you like to change through affirmations?

2. Perform the twenty-one day affirmation exercise and make daily notes on your progress.

Chapter V

The Law
Of
Human
Magnetism

The Fifth Universal Law of Success is the Universal Law of Human Magnetism. It is sometimes called the Universal Law of Radiation and Attraction. This law is stated in Galatians 6:7:

> "...for whatsoever a (person) soweth,
> that shall (they) also reap."

**A simple statement of the fifth universal law is:
Like Attracts Like.**

The basic principle of the Universal Law of Human Magnetism is that you attract what you are, and you are what you think about most of the time.

Each of us is a human magnet, attracting or repelling, like or unlike, thoughts, feelings, and associations into our life experience. This Universal Law of Radiation and Attraction reveals one of the fundamental principles of life—that life is lived from within, out. Whatever the vision of your desired life experience, it will only manifest when you feel, in your innermost feelings, that you are worthy of it. This desired outcome has its greatest impact when it is in harmony with your purpose.

"Feeling gets the blessing."
—Rev. Ike

Attitude

Your attitude is a form of human radiation which gives other people a perception and understanding of who you are, what you are about, and where you are going. It is a manner of feeling, acting, and thinking that shows your disposition, opinion, and personality. This instrument of communication is a moment-to-moment projection of your thoughts and feelings onto the world. Based on whatever you send out, the world responds to you. Your attitude is a powerful tool which can be used effectively to attract desired people, things, and circumstances into your life experience.

The two primary components of attitude are projection and perception.

Your self-image is communicated or projected to

others through your attitude. This communication projected by you is then perceived by others, and they respond accordingly. If you desire other people to be friendly, kind, and generous towards you, then you must project just those qualities in your attitude toward them. To use your attitude most effectively, you must recognize these two components and strive to make the projection and perception of your self-image one and the same.

The communication that you project through your attitude has two parts: the thoughts and images you project, and the feelings you have inside about those thoughts and images, which you also project.

When you interact with another person through your attitude, that person receives both parts of your communication. However, they perceive and usually respond to the feeling part, no matter what the thinking part says.

For example, you meet a new business associate who wants to impress you. He or she starts to share their ideas and vision which sound incredible. But, for some reason you have a gut feeling that this person is not all he or she claims to be. You respond accordingly with searching questions, looking for inconsistencies. Here, the ideas being projected by the new associate were not consistent with the feelings being perceived by you, and you reacted accordingly. Later, you usually find that your gut feeling was accurate.

When the attitude projected and perceived are one and the same, you become magnetic, attracting people and situations which will benefit you. If that same new associate had a different feeling inside about the thoughts being projected, then you would respond differently. If you felt nothing but sincerity, honesty, and a deep sense of commitment radiating from the new associate as he or she shared the same thoughts and vision in the first example, you would be the first to offer your support and help them in any way.

If you feel that most people seem to misunderstand you and your intentions most of the time, this could be a result of a contradiction between the thoughts and the feelings you project though your attitude.

There is no simple attitude projection or reception formula. How others respond to your attitude is a combination of what you are projecting in thoughts and feelings, and the state of mind of the perceiver, the other person.

Sometimes, there may be a misconception between what you believe you are projecting through your attitude, and what others are perceiving. This leads to the question that people often ask themselves: *"How could they treat me like this, as nice as I have been to them?"*

When this occurs, look both at the thoughts and feelings you are projecting, and the state of mind, or level of consciousness, of the person with whom you are dealing. Perhaps you are casting your pearls before swine. Or, maybe its you who needs an attitude adjustment.

Knowing that your attitude is a projection of the thoughts and feelings of your self-image onto the world, examine your inner thoughts (conscious mind) and your inner feelings (subconscious mind). If your inner thoughts and feelings are not in harmony with each other, there will be an inner tension which is reflected in your attitude.

For example, suppose your inner thoughts are focused on positive images of good health, happiness, prosperity, and love. And, your inner feelings are centered on ignorance, fear, and doubt, which were learned when you were younger. The results you get will be in accord with your feelings, not in accord with your thoughts. This indeed leads to tension and frustration.

How you feel is more powerful than what you think.

When your inner thoughts and inner feelings are in harmony, your self-image is intact. This harmonic self-image is then projected to others through your attitude with astoundingly positive results.

The nature of attitude is effective communication for mutual development and continuous growth. You acknowledge the value of another person's perception of your attitude based on their response. When their response is in harmony with your projected attitude, you have established the foundation for harmonic communication with that person and ultimately all humanity.

Overcoming Fear

Your attitude is like a great circle. There is a positive half and a negative half. The 180 degrees of the positive side represents a positive attitude, a positive thinker. The 180 degrees of the negative side represents a negative attitude, a negative thinker. The difference between the positive and negative thinker always lies in the feelings each has about themselves. The negative thinker's feelings are centered on ignorance, fear, and doubt. The positive thinker's feelings are centered on knowledge and understanding, courage and faith.

The negative thinker is motivated by six basic fears:

1. Fear of Poverty.

This is the fear of the loss of the tangible things you have acquired; the fear of going broke. People who fear poverty hoard money and material possessions. They are often cheap and stingy, even though they may possess great wealth. The fear of poverty will keep you broke in consciousness, regardless of what you may possess in your bank account. It destroys ambition, initiative, enthusiasm, persistence, and self-discipline. The fear of poverty invites failure at every turn.

2. Fear of Criticism.

This fear robs you of your initiative and destroys your power of imagination. It is usually fatal to your own personal achievement. The fear of criticism can induce inferiority complexes and virtually paralyze you. It makes you timid, insecure, and slow to reach decisions, or express opinions. The fear of criticism will make you an imitator instead of an innovator.

3. Fear of Ill Health.

The fear of ill health stems from negative knowledge and negative feelings about illness. It causes you to become preoccupied with symptoms of sickness and disease. The habit of constantly speaking and thinking with strong feelings about sickness and disease, often creates the very symptoms of the illness in your life experience. Disappointments in business and love affairs cause the fear of ill health to grow and magnify.

4. Fear of Loss of Love.

This fear is probably the most powerful of all the basic fears. The fear of the loss of love causes you to become suspicious of everyone. You quickly find fault with friends and loved ones, often without cause. It encourages the idea that love can be bought. People who fear the loss of love often give gifts at the slightest provocation. They also have a tendency to remind you of every good thing they have done—or think they have done—for you.

5. Fear of Old Age.

The fear of old age, to a large extent, stems from the negative portrayal we have as a society of the challenges of old age. This fear often manifests as a fear of being alone and unable to care for yourself. Sometimes the fear of poverty masquerades as a fear of old age. Here you believe that as you grow older, you are in greater danger of losing your worldly possessions. The fear of old age causes you to constantly talk about other people's age, or how good or bad they look for their age. The fear of old age will have you constantly apologizing for your age. It will drive you to try to dress, act, and look like a younger person. People who fear old age often try to associate themselves with younger people.

6. Fear of Death.

The fear of death comes from concentrating on dying instead of living. It often stems from idleness, lack of purpose, and lack of occupation. People who fear death are often the same ones who have wasted their lives in frivolous unproductive endeavors. This fear also comes from a sense of unfulfillment in those who live their lives without direction. The fear of poverty sometimes manifests as the fear of death. Here you feel that your death will inflict poverty or hardship upon your family and loved ones.

These six basic fears and their infamous cousins, *indecision* and *doubt*, go to the very heart of your feeling nature. When these fears hold you hostage, every thought or vision that you have in your conscious mind is neutralized. The results that you experience will be in harmony with these fears. As long as these fears control your feeling nature, your attitude cannot be positive. It will be counterproductive in pursuing your vision. The Universal Law of Radiation and Attraction will work against you.

The first step in adjusting your attitude is to realize that **all fears are simply states of the mind.** Since you can control your mind, you can overcome these fears by changing your thinking.

Eliminate the fear of poverty by refusing to accept any condition which leads to poverty. Refine your ability to handle money. Master money and possessions so that they can work for you, to confidently neutralize this fear of poverty. Learn to joyfully accept the wealth you acquire, realizing that this wealth is but a symbol of your thinking and the rewards of your efforts.

Erase the fear of criticism by refusing to worry about what other people think, say, or do. Know that you are doing the best you can, and that you will always get better.

Overcome the fear of ill health by forgetting

symptoms of illness, and replacing them with thoughts of good health.

Have no fear of losing love, because love cannot be lost. Love is an endless flow of feeling, seeking balance between the giver and the receiver.

Realize that old age is a great blessing which develops wisdom, understanding and discipline.

Release yourself from the fear of death by recognizing that death is just another transformation in the cycle of life, not an end.

The other negative emotion which can adversely affect your attitude is worry.

Worry

Worry is a negative state of mind which causes anxiety, distress, and uneasiness. It works slowly but persistently, destroying your initiative, self-confidence, and reasoning faculty.

Worry is a form of continuous fear caused by indecision or uncertainty with respect to the outcome of a particular situation, event or circumstance. It is a very real negative force which consumes and destroys all who come under its influence. Worry affects the circulation, the heart, the glands, the whole nervous system. More people die from worry than from overwork.

When your mind is filled with fear and worry, a negative vibration is transmitted. This vibration passes through your attitude to the minds of all who experience your presence. To eliminate worry, you must change your attitude towards its cause.

Eliminating Worry

The first and most important step toward eliminating worry is to kill the worry habit by making a blanket decision that *nothing in life is worth the price of worry.* This general decision symbolizes, in your own mind, a commitment not to yield to the pangs of worry, no matter what.

The second step is realize that no amount of worrying will change or help the outcome. Change your attitude toward the situation or condition causing you to worry. Change your attitude by changing your thinking and feelings about that which is causing you to worry. Replace negative thoughts and feelings of indecision, fear, and doubt with positive thoughts and feelings based on understanding, faith, and courage.

The third step to eliminating worry is to practice the following seven point formula for eliminating worry from your life.

The Seven Point Formula
for Eliminating Worry

1. Realize that most of the things you worry about will not happen. Montaigne, the French essayist, put it this way, *"My life has been filled with terrible misfortunes, most of which never happened."*

2. Determine the worst possible outcome of the situation you are worrying about. Once you know the worst that can happen, you can then face it.

3. Resolve to accept the worst if it happens.

4. Proceed to improve upon the worst by concentrating on the positive aspects of the situation. You can pierce through visions and appearances created by fear to truth revealed by understanding and self-confidence. Very often, what appears to be an invincible monster of negativity, upon closer inspection, becomes a coward whose only source of strength is darkness and fear.

5. Review your life experiences, especially those which worked for you in the past. Concentrate on lessons you have learned which can be helpful in resolving the current situation. Look for instances in which you overcame some obstacles, or completed an important assignment. Each success builds your faith in yourself and in your abilities.

Where faith prevails, worry must flee.

6. Practice living one day at a time. Live in day-tight compartments. Forget yesterday's failures and tomorrow's possibilities for success. Concentrate on doing everything you can today to make tomorrow the way you want it to be.

7. Do not cross the bridge until you get there. Take care of today; tomorrow will take care of itself. Do not waste your energies dealing with situations which may arise in the future. Taking good care of the present will often resolve or dissolve potential future situations automatically.

Enthusiasm

Enthusiasm is one of your most important assets. It is an infectious state of mind which gets for you the cooperation of other people, attracting them to your way of thinking and acting. When you are enthusiastic about where you are going, people notice it and make way for you. In fact, the world makes way for those who know where they are going.

According to the dictionary, enthusiasm means: *"to be inspired; possessed by god; intense or eager interest; zeal."* It comes from the Greek roots en/theos, meaning God within. In ancient times, enthusiasm was associated with supernatural inspiration or possession. This supernatural aspect was a result of the infectious nature of enthusiasm in attracting the attention and cooperation of others.

Enthusiasm operates as an invisible and powerful force of human magnetism, attracting or repelling that which you desire in your life experience. Thus, it is a powerful force at your command, eager to carry out your wishes and fed by the thoughts you hold constantly in your mind.

Types of Enthusiasm

There are two types of enthusiasm: animated enthusiasm and genuine enthusiasm.
Each type is related to the source of motivation which stimulates its existence.
There are two primary sources of motivation: external and internal.
External motivation manifests as fear motivation or reward motivation. As children, fear and reward are our

first motivational experiences.

Internal motivation manifests as self-motivation or spiritual motivation. We develop internal motivation as we become older and more knowledgeable.

Animated enthusiasm is based on external motivation. It is a created or manufactured emotion which is stimulated by fear or reward. In other words, you pretend or act enthusiastic based on your knowledge, experience, or belief that it will work for you.

Genuine enthusiasm is based on internal motivation. It can be created by animated enthusiasm which is consistently and continuously exercised. When you act enthusiastically, you are enthusiastic. Acting and becoming occur simultaneously.

The magnetic power of enthusiasm is effective regardless of whether it is animated or genuine. The relationship between animated and genuine enthusiasm is like that of the natural magnetism of magnetite (iron) found in the earth, and artificially induced magnetism which results from passing an electric current through certain metals (an electromagnet).

The power of human magnetism is that its natural source is under your control, within your own thoughts and consciousness. When you create enthusiasm by intentionally acting enthusiastic, you are priming your pump. Once you get totally into the *"part,"* or vision, you wish to project, your affected enthusiasm becomes genuine. Your human magnetism then springs from the internal consciousness of self and God. The strength of this magnetism is based on the level of your self-confidence, and the quality of your faith and relationship with God.

Generating Enthusiasm

Enthusiasm is one of your important success habits. You should make a habit of doing everything with eagerness, class, and style. A high level of enthusiasm should be demonstrated in everything you do.

Nothing is so unimportant as to do it without enthusiasm. When you act enthusiastically, you are enthusiastic.

Manifestations of Enthusiasm

Your enthusiasm is manifested in every aspect of your being. It is in the sound of your voice, your tone, your motion and movements, and the look in your eyes. Enthusiasm is shown by your walk, your gait, the way you shake hands and hold your head and mouth. It should express itself as an intense eagerness for life and living.

Walk through the world like a champion, with class and style.

How to Generate Enthusiasm

1. Have a great sense of expectancy each day.

Maintain a *"great day"* attitude in all that you do. Constantly say to yourself, *"This is a great day for work, sharing and being happy."* When you project a *great day* attitude, you radiate a positive magnetic force which will attract a *great day* into your experience of life. Things seem to go your way. You are in the right place at the right time. People and things you are looking for appear just when you need them. Your sense of expectancy becomes a blueprint for your day.

That which you expect and project, with feeling, you attract. Each day brings you that which you ask of it.

2. Realize that you can control your mind, your thoughts, your feelings and emotions, and your actions.

You are the captain of your ship and the master of your destiny. No one and nothing can take control of your mind unless you permit it. Remember, you are both the gardener and the garden. Weeds, negative unproductive thoughts and feelings, can only grow if you let them. When you let weeds grow in the garden that is your life, either by doing nothing or by doing ineffective things, you have given up control of your life.

Take control of your thoughts and your feelings, for they are the blueprints of your life.

You become what you think about most of the time.

3. Realize that any state of mind is contagious.

The nature and quality of your thoughts represent your state of mind. Your state of mind, as projected through your attitude, is a powerful force. It influences and interacts with the state of mind of others. If your state of mind is negative, you radiate a negative attitude to others, who will respond accordingly. A positive state of mind will radiate a positive attitude which will influence others to respond favorably, attracting them to your way of thinking and acting.

4. Realize that your personal appearance presents a picture of who you are, what you are about, and where

you are going.

Your physical appearance is a primary manifestation of your state of mind. You cannot deceive your own thoughts. What you physically appear to be in reality, is in fact the physical representation of the nature and quality of your state of mind.

5. Maintain a constant level of enthusiasm at all times.

Some people constantly fluctuate from the heights of enthusiasm to the depths of negativity. This fluctuation results from their inner thoughts and inner feelings being inconsistent with, and out of harmony with, each other. Strive to maintain a balanced, harmonic state of mind, centered on positive thoughts of work, love, sharing, and joy. A balanced, positive state of mind never runs out of enthusiasm.

Chapter Summary

The Universal Law of Human Magnetism states that you attract what you are, and you are what you think about most of the time. This universal law operates through a process of radiation and attraction. Each of us is like a magnet radiating a form of energy which attracts or repels—like or unlike—thoughts, feelings, and associations. Human magnetism operates primarily through your attitude and your enthusiasm.

Your attitude projects who you are, what you are

about, and where you are going. It may either be positive or negative. When it is positive, you project knowledge, understanding, courage, and faith. When it is negative, you project ignorance, fear, and doubt. The primary manifestation of a negative attitude is fear.

Enthusiasm is one of your most important assets. It gets for you the cooperation of other people, attracting them to your way of thinking and acting.

Study Guide

1. Are you surrounded by people who consistently misunderstand you?

2. What are you projecting in your attitude that attracts these people into your space?

3. Do you have fears that impact your success journey? What are they?

4. How can you overcome these fears?

5. What can you do to be more enthusiastic about your life? About your job? About your relationships?

Chapter VI

The Law
Of
Focus

The Sixth Universal Law of Success is the Universal Law of Focus and Discipline. This universal law provides that your attention must always be focused on your goals, vision, and purpose; and your thoughts, emotions, and actions must always be under your control.

> *"The light of the body is in the eye:*
> *if thine eye be single,*
> *thy whole body shall be full of light."*
> —Matthew 6:22

Metaphysically, this means that understanding, knowledge, and wisdom (light), comes through what you see—that to which you give your attention. If you focus your attention *(thine eye be single)*, on that which you endeavor to accomplish, then it shall be accomplished on its grandest scale. The more focused you are, the more successful you will become.

To be focused means to exert such self-control that no one and nothing can deter or distract you from your goals and your vision.

The Power of Focus

Wherever you place your focus, your thoughts, emotions, and even events and activities will follow. For example, race car drivers are taught to focus on where they want the car to go. When a race car goes into a spin, the driver's tendency is to focus on the wall rather than the center of the track. If they focus on the wall, that is usually what they hit. As a result, drivers are taught not to focus on the wall, but rather to focus on where they want the car to go. When they do this, they have a far better chance of avoiding the wall and coming out of the spin.

Applying the law of thought:

*What you recognize (focus on),
you energize (in your feeling nature).
What you energize, you realize (results).*

If you focus on a problem, rather than the solution to that problem, you will never solve or overcome it. However, if you focus on solving the problem, the solution will appear.

To be focused requires faith in yourself and your abilities. If you have no faith in yourself, you cannot be focused.

If you are confronted with the problem of lack of money, focusing on this problem—lack of money—you will always be broke. If you change your perspective and focus on the solution—new and better ways to bring more money into your hands—and have faith in yourself and in your money generating ideas, money-substance will come to you.

How To Overcome Lack of Focus

1. Realize that you can only focus on one thing at a time.

Focus is like a laser beam, rather than a light bulb. It cuts through the darkness and illuminates one thought, emotion, activity, or thing at a time.

2. Be in good health, physically fit, and full of energy.

Health challenges can demand your immediate, consistent, and continuous attention. When you are not physically fit and full of energy, the lack of stamina and feelings of tiredness will consume your mind. Your primary thoughts will be focused on resting and sleeping.

> *"He who has health, has hope;*
> *and he who has hope, has everything."*
> —Arabian Proverb

3. Have clearly defined goals which complement your vision and life purpose.

Without clearly defined goals there is no direction or thought on which to focus your attention. There are no flowers to plant in the garden that is your life; and thus, weeds—uncontrolled emotions and instincts—will grow.

4. Have faith in yourself and your abilities.

Faith gives power to focus. When you focus on ideas and thoughts, they become the *"substance of things hoped for, the evidence of things not seen."*

Conceive (Focus) + Believe (Faith) =
Achieve (Results)

5. Realize that all distractions are equal, and equally counterproductive.

Keep your eye on the prize—your goals, vision, and purpose. Anything, any thought, any person, and any emotion that is not supportive of and congruent with your goals, vision, and purpose is a distraction

6. Control your body, instincts, and emotions.

Your instincts and emotions are forces driven by your lower, animal nature. You must take possession of your mind in such strength or degree that your emotions, your instincts and your body are under your control.

The Saboteur Within

Often, when you begin your journey on the path, there appears to be a negative part of you that works against the positive things you attempt to do. It is in disharmony with the positive part of you which pursues your goals, vision, and purpose. This negative part of you functions as a saboteur in all your endeavors.

The tools of this saboteur are distractions, discouragement, distrust, doubt, indecision, procrastination, apathy, arrogance, isolation, and low self-esteem. This saboteur is neutralized by constantly focusing your attention, your actions, and your feelings, on your goals, vision, and purpose. To focus your attention, your actions, and your feelings, requires self-discipline or self-control.

Self-Discipline

To have self-control or self-discipline, means that you have taken possession of your mind in such strength or degree that your emotions, your instincts, and your body are under your control. Self-discipline is control from within.

Your self-discipline begins with your thoughts. If you cannot control your thoughts, you cannot control your actions or your emotions. When you have control over your thoughts, you can never be mastered by others. You will always be able to take possession of whatever you are entitled to or deserve.

Anger

One of the main causes of loss of focus is the emotion of anger. When someone makes you angry, they have taken control of your mind. Being angry means somebody else is pulling your strings. Do not give in to the feelings and thoughts of anger. Always be positive.

It is difficult to be angry with a smile on your face.

When people attempt to make you angry, smile, whistle, and say *"ain't it great—fantastic."* They may think you are a little strange, but they will carry their negativity elsewhere.

To be in control, you must always be positive. Stay as far away from all negativity as possible over the next six months, and watch the change this brings about in your life.

Although you may not be able to control the acts of other people, you can control your own reactions to those acts. In fact, other people cannot take control of your life at all. You must give it to them. If you do not give control of your mind to another person, letting them make you angry, they have no power over you.

> *"He is a fool who cannot be angry;*
> *but he is a wise man who will not."*
> —Old Proverb

True wisdom comes only through self-understanding based on self-discipline. When you have self-discipline, discipline from outside is unnecessary. You are then your own boss, the captain of your ship. Your own initiative causes you to get a job done or a task completed.

When you live without discipline,
You die without dignity.

Seven Ways to Improve Your Self-Discipline

1. Believe that you can succeed and set about

doing just that.

First and foremost, you must have complete faith in your abilities, and courage to take immediate action.

2. Learn to roll with the punches.

Do not give in to pressures. Don't sweat the small stuff. If you take care of the big things, the little things will take care of themselves.

3. Get busy achieving your goals.

If you just do it, get busy following your plans and achieving your goals, you will soon forget why they cannot be done.

4. Always be aware of the positive elements of hope.

Do not get into a rut. Hope is life and life is hope.

5. Have complete confidence in your ability to find a solution to any situation or circumstance.

Know that you know that you know. Know that there is always a solution. Reformulate the situation or circumstance in a way that facilitates solution or resolution. For example, if you are faced with a difficult task, ask yourself, *"How can I complete this task and enjoy the experience?"*

6. Keep going and growing.

Be excited about your own performance each day. Affirm, *"Everyday in everyway I am getting better."*

7. Be a self-starter.

Do it now. Do not procrastinate. Don't wait for someone else to ring your bell. Be self-motivated. Start each day with a winning attitude.

Chapter Summary

The Universal Law of Focus and Discipline states that your attention must always be focused on your goals, vision, and purpose. Your thoughts, emotions, and actions must always be under control. Self-discipline is the process by which you maintain your focus. It is a learned behavior which must be developed and perfected. When you have self-discipline, discipline from outside is unnecessary.

Study Guide

1. What steps are you taking to stay focused on your goals and your vision?

2. Is there any one particular thing that distracts you from pursuing your goals?

3. Why and how does it distract you?

4. Are you satisfied with your level of self-discipline?

5. What can you do to improve your self-discipline?

Chapter VII

The Law
Of
Action

The Seventh Universal Law of Success is the Law of Action. This universal law governs the manner or method of performing the activities of life. It is the methodology by which the principles of success are actually implemented on a day-to-day, moment-to-moment basis. The law of action encompasses your behavior, conduct, habits, and method of operation. It is the operating process by which your thoughts and feelings become the things and experiences of your life.

> *"But be ye doers of the word,*
> *and not hearers only,*
> *deceiving your own selves."*
>
> —James 1:22

All that is written in this book and in all other instruments of enlightenment are absolutely worthless unless you put these ideas and principles into action.

On a practical level, the Universal Law of Action focuses on the following:

1. The work (employment) you perform for material survival.
2. Planning your actions to produce desired results.
3. Achieving your goals and vision of life.
4. Overcoming obstacles and challenges that confront you.

Right Work

Work is generally defined as a means to earn a living. In a broader sense, work is the physical or mental effort or activity directed toward producing or accomplishing a desired result.

If I ask the question, *"Why do you work?"*, most people will give the same basic answer—to make a living.

What are you getting out of your work? Generally, the objective of the physical and mental activity of getting up each morning, getting dressed, and rushing to your place of employment, is to obtain the money to meet the material requirements of your life. If all that you are getting out of work is the financial wherewithal to take care of yourself, then you are being grossly underpaid, no matter how much you make.

As long as the objective of your work is something outside yourself, you are being shortchanged.

When you think of work as something external, to obtain external objectives, you are cutting yourself off from the true meaning and essence of work. In fact, as long as you consider work as an external endeavor, you will delay your success in life.

Work must be considered on an internal, spiritual level. It should not be seen as a *"means to make a living"*, but rather as a *"means to live your making"*. Your work should be an external expression of your internal state of being or level of consciousness. Work should be a means by which you can express your internal good desires, and which provides the required material substance to maintain and enhance the conditions of your life.

Work has a divine, spiritual nature which, when properly attuned, can put you in harmony with the cosmic flow of good, success, and everlasting reward. When your work does this, it is your *"right work"*.

How do you find your *"right work"*?

Make the most of your present situation. Develop a positive wholesome attitude toward work in general, and specifically toward the work you are doing right now.

Sometimes, you find yourself working at something you do not particularly care for, when you are just getting started in your working career, or while you are near the bottom of the success ladder. However, it is your attitude and reaction to your work at this point which determines if you will continue at the bottom, or move up the success ladder. If you constantly complain about your present work, blaming yourself and others for your condition, you will probably not progress much further. You will go from job to job, always unhappy, always complaining and never progressing.

If you take charge of your attitude, and condition it to seeing the good and positive aspects of your present work situation, then you are laying the spiritual foundation for positive change toward your *"right work"*. Recognize that your present work is for a purpose. Believe that this purpose is to develop divine qualities of patience, persistence, understanding, and discipline. These qualities will lead you to your *"right work"*.

When you look at your work as an external expression of your internal desires, then you must do your very best in performing this work for your desires to be fulfilled. This is the principle of work stated in the Bible:

> *"Whatsoever thy hand findeth to do,*
> *do it with (all) thy might . . ."*
> —Ecclesiastes 9:10

If you hold back on your work, then you also hold back on the fulfillment of your internal desires.

At the beginning stages of your success journey, your internal desires may not be clearly defined in your conscious mind. It is through this principle of work that your internal desires are revealed to you. Give your body, mind, and spirit to your work, believing that it is for a divine purpose. This committed action will guide you to your *"right work"*, and ultimately to your life purpose.

Evaluating Your Present Position

When you work, have a goal and vision in your mind. Think of how you want your life to be, what you want to do, and what you want to have. Define your goals and vision clearly and concisely in your thoughts. That which you establish in your thoughts becomes the blueprint for your life experience.

When your energies, through work, are directed toward specific goals, you create a positive forward momentum. This forward momentum helps you overcome the things you dislike about your present work situation.

If you are not satisfied with your present work situation, focus your attention on your goals and proceed toward them. Determine what you must do to move closer to your goals. If you need more education or experience, be willing to get it. By focusing on your goals and vision, you are less affected by the conditions of your present work situation.

Many people, though they are dissatisfied with their work, will not put forth the extra effort to pursue their goals and vision. They become satisfied with their dissatisfaction. They prefer to complain and criticize others rather than take steps to change or improve their condition. These unfortunate souls become so overwhelmed with the weeds—the negative aspects of their present work situation—that they hide their own shortcomings and dissatisfaction by criticizing and tearing down other people.

To attain your *"right work"*, you must remove the weeds and avoid this kind of negative conduct. Believe in your heart that no set of conditions or circumstances can keep you from attaining your goals and realizing your vision. Take the high road and rise above the shortcomings of your present work to the foundation of your *"right work"*, as revealed by your goals and vision.

Once you establish your vision and your goals, you can properly *examine your present work situation in terms of the following three standards:*

1. Reasonable pay for your present living circumstances.
2. Knowledge, experience and training that will be valuable to you in the future.
3. Prestige, contacts, and acquaintances who can be of assistance in attaining your goals and realizing your vision.

Evaluate your present work situation, and any other position you consider taking, in terms of these three standards. The most important of these standards is the second one—valuable knowledge, experience, and training. The next in importance is prestige, contacts and acquaintances. Reasonable pay for the present is the least important of all. This is not to imply that reasonable pay is not important, because it is. The point is, if a sacrifice is to be made, do it in the present. Beware of urges for immediate gratification and consumption.

Do not sacrifice the future to satisfy the present.

Success Planning

The goals you set for yourself should represent your vision and your deep desires in life. Whether you realize your vision depends on your ability to systematically and consistently attain your underlying goals. The most important element in attaining your goals is the formation and execution of definite, practical plans which work.

*A success plan is an organized course of action
which allows you to produce desired results.*

The desired result to be produced is the attainment of your goals and the realization of your vision. Producing results reflects your ability to organize your time, plan your work, and work your plan. To construct a great skyscraper requires an accurate blueprint, which is diligently followed by the builders.This blueprint is a tangible representation of the vision of the skyscraper in the mind of the architect.

Your success plan is the blueprint of your own vision. It is a tangible representation of the ideas and thoughts which make up your vision. If you diligently follow your success plan, you will get the desired results, attain your goals, and realize your vision.

Constantly monitor the productiveness of your plan. Evaluate the productiveness of your plan on a daily basis. If your plan works, double your efforts for even greater results. Do not waste time on a plan that does not work. If your plan does not lead you on a continuous, step-by-step journey toward your goals, replace it with a new plan. If the new plan does not work either, replace it with still another plan. Continue to monitor and evaluate your plan until you find one that works for you. Give each plan sufficient opportunity to produce desired results.

Pay special attention to your own efforts in executing each plan. Be sure to put in enough time and energy to give your plan a reasonable opportunity to work and produce desired results. Very often you will find that your plan is sound, but it requires more time, energy, expertise, and resources to make it work. Then, it is up to you.

Are you willing to increase your own commitment

for your success? Or will you look for a plan that requires a lesser commitment of time, energy, expertise, and resources? The fact is, when you increase your commitment to your goals, you are looking toward success. But, when you accept a lesser commitment, you are heading for failure.

When your commitment is high, and you're willing to give even more, and yet your plan fails, ditch it and get a new plan. Give your best efforts to make each plan work, and don't be discouraged by temporary failure. Most people experience failure because they are not persistent in developing new plans to replace those which do not work.

What can you do to make a success plan, and accomplish the objectives of your plan?

The Nine Step Method to Make a Success Plan.

1. Purchase a daily planner.
Live by the book. Your planner should be the official daily record of your journey *on the path*—your success journey.

2. Write your vision, goals, and target dates in your planner.

3. List the actions necessary to accomplish your goals, and when they must be performed.

4. Write out a brief, but complete narrative statement of how you intend to achieve your goals.
This is your success plan.

Writing Your Success Plan

a. I must accomplish the following goals:
(list goals)_____

b. In order to accomplish (my goals,) I must do the following:
(actions)_____by (dates)_____

c. The most important things that must be done to accomplish my goals are:
(goal #1)_____ (actions)_____
(goal #2)_____ (actions)_____

d. The order of importance in executing the actions:
(action#1)_____first on (date#1)_____
(action#2)_____second on (date#2)_____

e. The tools, materials, resources, or supplies I will need to accomplish my goals are:
#1._____
#2._____

f. The necessary tools, materials, resources, and supplies will be obtained in the following manner:
#1_____on or before (date#1)_____
#2_____on or before (date#2)_____

5. Revise, study, digest, and memorize your success plan statement.

6. Start right away doing the most important things first, then proceeding to lesser important ones.

7. Develop a daily timetable showing all actions to be performed and the dates they must be done.

8. Plan all actions that must be performed each day.

If you fail to perform an action on the day scheduled, move it over to the next day. Merge it in with the actions to be performed that day, in accord with its priority with respect to the actions already scheduled for that day.

9. Monitor your efforts closely and evaluate your results.

Concentrate on your plan of action. Act on it. Follow your timetable. Do not think that only you can perform the actions in your plan. Have other people do things for you. *Do not spend dollar time on penny jobs.* Do all of the important things first and plan to succeed.

Achieving Your Goals

Successful living depends on your ability to identify what you want, your vision for yourself, and then go after it. Once you determine your life vision and your long range goals, you can set annual, monthly, weekly, and daily goals which will lead you to your long-range goals.

Formula for Achieving Your Goals

1. Set a goal for one year.

Write each goal where you can see it many times a day. Place copies of your written goal in your wallet, on your mirror, on the door of your refrigerator, anywhere that you will see it often during the day. Read it over at least three times per day. Be sure to include the date you wish to accomplish your goal in your written statement.

2. Determine what must be done to accomplish your goal.

Write down each and every thing that must be done to guide you to your goal. Be very specific and detailed. List the things that must be done in the order of their importance. Write the date each activity must be started, and when it must be completed.

3. Set monthly goals that will lead you to your full- year goal.

Make the list of things that must be done to accomplish your full-year goal and arrange them by date to be completed. Review this date/priority list and write down what must be done each month to guide you to your full year goal. The items listed for each month become the basis for your monthly goals for each of the twelve months of the year.

4. Determine what you must do to accomplish each monthly goal.

Focus on your first month's goals. Organize the items necessary to accomplish your first month's goals by date to be accomplished and priority.

5. Set weekly goals for the first month.

The list by date and priority of the items necessary to accomplish your first month's goals become the basis for your weekly goals. Analyze this list by date to be started, date to be completed, and priority of importance. Considering the dates to be completed, write out the most important things to be accomplished each week of the first month. Focus on the first week of the first month.

6. Determine what must be done to accomplish the goals of the first week of the first month.

Analyze the first week's goals in great detail. Determine each and every action that must be performed to accomplish your first week's goals. List the actions by priority and date to be accomplished.

7. Set daily goals for the first week of the first month.

Based on the list of things to be done to accomplish your weekly goals, set daily goals which will lead you to your weekly goals.

8. Determine what actions must be performed each day to accomplish your daily goals.

List each day's required activities in the order of their importance. Do the most important things first.

9. Keep a record of your achievement.

Cross off each item on your daily list as you complete it. Try to complete everything on your list for each day. If you do not complete everything on your list for a particular day, carry the items not completed over to the next day and merge them in with the things to be done that day.

10. Learn from past failures, but do not let them slow you down.

If you find that you are not accomplishing the daily tasks you set for yourself, do not be discouraged. Analyze each day's activities and determine what is slowing you down. Devise a plan to improve your performance and implement it right away.

11. Avoid wasting time.

Time cannot be repeated or replaced. The main obstacle to completing each day's activities is improper use of your time. Each moment you should ask yourself, *"What is the best use of my time right now?"* Then, act accordingly.

12. Repeat this procedure without fail.

Repeat this weekly routine for each week of the first month, revising and improving as required. Evaluate your performance at the end of each week and resolve to do better. Follow the same procedure for each month of the year. Constantly revising and improving your performance, you will grow in faith and self-confidence.

13. Stick to your goal until it is accomplished.

A winner never quits, and a quitter never wins.

Whether you attain your goals or not is in your hands. If you refuse to accept failure, no matter what, you will succeed.

> *"If you think you are beaten, you are.*
> *If you think you dare not, you don't.*
> *If you like to win, but think you can't*
> *It's almost certain you won't.*

If you think you are outclassed, you are.
You've got to think high and rise.
You've got to be sure of yourself,
Before you can ever win a prize.

Life's battles don't always go
to the stronger or faster man.
But soon or later the man who wins,
Is the man who thinks he can."
                              —C. W. Longnecker

How To Overcome Obstacles

After you make your plans and start executing them, situations often develop which appear to be obstacles. When they appear, do not be discouraged or intimidated.

Don't let the appearance of an obstacle create an atmosphere for failure.

When an obstacle appears, do not see it as an impediment to your progress. See it as a challenge to your resources. *Convert stumbling blocks into stepping stones.*

To change obstacles into challenges, you must change your attitude toward the particular situation. Do not let your first thought or reaction to a situation be a negative one. Eliminate the words *obstacles* and *problem* from your vocabulary and from your thinking. Every experience that you encounter is a situation. Regardless of whether it is a positive or negative one, it is indeed a situation which can be resolved.

With this change in attitude toward the situations you

encounter, you are better equipped to handle them by seeing them as opportunities for completion or growth, rather than as impediments to progress.

One very effective method to overcome obstacles, resolve situations, and convert stumbling blocks into stepping stones is the following nine point formula for situation resolution.

The Nine Point Formula for Situation Resolution

1. Write it down.

Write a precise statement of the situation to be resolved. State what it is and what it is not. Very often, simply writing and describing the situation helps resolve it. Once you clearly define the situation, its solution starts rushing toward you.

2. Analyze the situation.

Look at the situation from all possible angles. Identify all aspects, paying particular attention to which portions can be resolved immediately, and which portions require further analysis.

3. List all alternative solutions.

Write each potential solution as completely as possible.

4. Evaluate all possible solutions.

Determine whom or what does each solution help, and whom or what does it hurt.

5. Determine if your solution (choice) is a selfish one.

If a potential solution helps only you, or hurts other people, it will probably cause you more difficulty in the future. Look for a solution that fairly balances the benefits to yourself and to others.

6. Picture the consequences.

Carry each possible solution to its logical conclusion. See the end results clearly and in great detail.

7. Get advice, but make the decision your own.

Discuss the situation with people you trust and respect. Ask for their insight and advice. Study their advice in conjunction with your own understanding and observations. Then, make the final decision your own.

8. Stick to your decision.

Once you make a decision, stick to it until new facts are produced warranting a change.

9. Put your decision into action immediately.

Do not procrastinate once you have made a decision. Get started right away and give it your best.

The nine point formula gives you a step by step method to improve the execution of your plans. Through this procedure, you can effectively convert stumbling blocks into stepping stones and provide yourself with golden opportunities to build faith and self- confidence.

Chapter Summary

The Universal Law of Action sets forth the methodology by which the principles of success are actually implemented on a day-to-day basis. It is the operating procedure by which your thoughts and feelings become the things and experiences of your life.

A success plan is an organized course of action which allows you to produce desired results. It is the blueprint of your vision. Your success plan is developed using the nine step procedure. Once your success plan is made, follow the thirteen step process to attain your goals.

Eliminate the words obstacle and problem from your vocablulary and from your thinking. Situations or challenges which arise in the execution of your plan may be handled through a systematic process of situation resolution.

Study Guide

1. What steps, if any, are you taking to identify your *"right work"*?

2. Write out your success plan for accomplishing your primary goals.

3. Take one of your goals and apply the goal achieving formula to determine what actions you must take this week towards accomplishing that goal.

4. Is there a primary challenge or situation keeping you from achieving your goals? If so, how will you overcome that challenge or situation?

Chapter VIII

The Law
Of
Value

The Eighth Universal Law of Success is the Universal Law of Value and Mutual Exchange.

"Give not that which is holy unto the dogs,
neither cast ye your pearls before swine,
lest they trample them under their feet,
and turn again and rend (tear) you."
—Matthew 7:6

The Universal Law of Value and Mutual Exchange covers the interactions that take place between the different levels of consciousness. When you, on one level of consciousness, interact with another person, that person should be on a level of consciousness commensurate with your own. All things have a level of consciousness.

Simply stated, the Universal Law of Value directs you not to waste your treasures—the things that are important to you—on people, places, or things that are beneath your level of consciousness.

For example, suppose you share your values of fairness, honesty, and truthfulness with another person who has the consciousness of a liar and a thief. That other person will hate and resent you. It will be only a matter of time before that other person responds to you and your values in the only way he or she can—by lying, cheating, and stealing from you.

It does not matter how much you love or care about that person, he or she can only respond to you in a manner consistent with their own level of consciousness—that of a liar and a thief.

The Universal Law of Value Has Four Main Aspects: time, thoughts, actions, and substance.

It states the following:

Do not waste your time on thoughts, people, or actions which are not worthy.

Do not waste your thoughts on ideas that are not worthy.

Do not waste your energies on activities which are not worthy.

Do not waste your money on that which is not worthy.

Do not waste your assets and talents on that which is not worthy of your attention, based on your goals, vision, and purpose. In making a value judgment or decision for allocating your assets and talents, always see your options in terms of their overall effect on your goals, vision and purpose.

Time

Your time, the hours you spend on this earth, is your most valuable asset. It is unrepeatable and irreplaceable. How you spend the hours you have been allotted in your life will determine the level of success you experience. You waste time when you spend it in unproductive endeavors or with unproductive people. The result of wasting your time quickly manifests in your life experience.

A better way to look at how to allocate your time is to speak in terms of investing your time, rather than spending it. To spend has a connotation of finality, with no return. When time is spent, it is gone forever. When time is invested, there is a sense of return on the investment. For example, if you spend time in college, you may or may not graduate. However, if you invest time in college, it seems to be a natural result that you graduate.

The Universal Law of Value says: invest your time only in those people and those activities which are congruent with, or harmonic with, your goals and vision. Choose to deal primarily with those people who are on a comparable level of consciousness with you. This is not to negate the value of charity work with people who are less fortunate or on a lower level of consciousness. The point is that you recognize it as charity work, and allocate your time and energy accordingly.

Ask yourself the time question, *"What is the best use of my time right now?"* Or, more precisely, *"What is the best use of my time right now, taking into consideration my goals, vision, and purpose?"*

Thoughts

Your thoughts are the blueprints for your reality. If you entertain thoughts which are beneath your level of consciousness, then you are wasting your incredible thought capacity on unworthy exercises.

Great minds discuss ideas.
Average minds discuss places and things.
Small minds discuss other people.

The Universal Law of Thought provides,

You become what you think
about most of the time.

Do not fill your mind with thoughts that are below the type and nature of thoughts you are capable of thinking or should be thinking. Otherwise, these lower thoughts will manifest in your life. Even if you permit yourself to think lower thoughts in jest, or unintentionally, the subconscious mind accepts as true whatever thought—intentional or unintentional—is in your mind. It then proceeds to objectify that thought it in your life experience.

Do not permit lower, unproductive thoughts which do not support your goals and purpose to occupy your mind. If you pay attention to these lower, unproductive thoughts, you will not achieve your goals and purpose. In fact, you will be laying the foundation for your own failure in the not too distant future.

Ask yourself the mind question, *"What is the best use of my mind right now, taking into consideration my goals, vision, and purpose?"*

Actions

Your actions are the bridges between your thoughts and your reality. Do not spend time on frivolous, unproductive activities. Any activity that is not in furtherance of your goals, vision, and purpose is a frivolous and unproductive one.

Ask yourself the action question, *"What is the most effective thing I can do right now, that will lead me to my goals, my vision, and my purpose?*

Money

"Money is the getting potential of your self-image."
—Dr. Johnnie Colemon

It may be measured in currency or in results. The lack or shortage of money is one of the main excuses unsuccessful people give for not being more successful.

To understand the law of value as applied to money, let us first examine the principles of money and wealth.

The Four Principles of Wealth

1. The Earning Principle.
All wealth is created in the mind. The earning principle covers the exchange of value required to create sufficient income to meet your needs.

2. The Spending Principle.
The spending principle covers the manner in which you spend, circulate, or otherwise dispose of your money.

3. The Savings Principle.
The savings principle covers the accumulation of surplus—the difference between your income and expenses—from your income.

4. The Investing Principle.
The investing principle covers the allocation of surplus to increase your wealth and income.

The Universal Law of Value as applied to money is as follows: Generate sufficient income in a manner that supports your goals. Wisely exchange your time, knowledge, and energies to generate this income. Spend this income in a manner consistent with your goals, which empowers you and others. Pay yourself first as a means to create a surplus—your savings. Put a portion of your savings to work in a self-generating investment, which itself produces growth and income.
Put simply:

Spend less than you earn. Save what you do not spend. Invest a portion of what you save to help you generate more.

Ask yourself the money question, *"What is the best use of my money right now, in terms of my goals, vision, and purpose?."*

Mastering the Riddle of Survival

As you progress along *the path*, you become keenly aware of how much time and effort is devoted to generating sufficient income to meet the needs of you and your family. This challenge of your financial survival is an important test of your knowledge, skill, determination, and self-discipline.

If you do not meet this challenge and master it, you put a severe limitation on your ability to achieve your goals and realize your purpose. In fact, as long as you are living paycheck to paycheck, or are dependent on someone or something for assistance, you will find it difficult to give the time and focus your attention with enough intensity to get desired results. So, it is crucial that you meet and overcome this financial challenge, and thereby solve the riddle of survival.

To solve the riddle of survival means that you have achieved a level of financial independence in which the fruits of your labors are sufficient that you can continue to live indefinitely at a level which is pleasing to you, without any further effort required.

For example, suppose you conclude that $36,000 per year would be sufficient to meet all of your financial needs. Your objective is to devise a plan to generate sufficient assets and/or wealth to produce an annual income or $36,000, without touching the principal.

How to Create Wealth

There are three basic ways to create wealth:

1. Wages and salaries
2. Income from a business
3. Income from investments

Take a very common scenario. You are forty years old. You don't own a business. You have no investments. But, you have a good job paying you $36,000 per year. What can you do, and how long will it take for you to accumulate enough wealth or assets to guarantee yourself $36,000 per year income for life? Assume that you decide to create this wealth by taking advantage of the power of compound interest over time. And further assume that you chose to invest monthly in a mutual fund.

First, determine how much wealth or assets in mutual funds you would have to accumulate to generate $36,000 per year income. Assuming an annual return of 12%, which is fairly conservative, it would take:

$$\$36,000/12\% \ = \ \$36,000/.12 = \$300,000$$

A $300,000 principal investment in a mutual fund at 12% annual return would give you a $36,000 income per year for life.

Using the standard compound interest tables available at most banks, mutual funds or libraries, you can see how much you will have in ten to thirty years at various monthly investment amounts.

Compound Interest Projection Table

Invest Monthly	Accumulated Dollar Amount		
	10 Yrs.	20 Yrs.	30 Yrs.
$100	$23,004	$98,924	$349,496
$200	$46,008	$197,848	$698,992
$300	$69,012	$296,772	$1,048,488

Always pay yourself first. If you take 10% of your annual income and invest it in monthly installments, you would be investing:

10% of $36,000 = $3,600 per year
$3,600/12 months = $300 per month.

From the compound interest table you will see that if you invest $300 per month in a mutual fund earning 12% per year, you would have $296,772 in twenty years. In other words, you would have mastered the riddle of survival at age sixty. If you get started sooner or increase your monthly investment, you will achieve this independence much sooner. If, for instance, you started this program at age thirty, you would be there at age fifty.

This example shows that you do not need a big inheritance, special talents, or contacts. You can solve the riddle of survival yourself over time with self-discipline.

Another approach to solving the riddle of survival is to establish or purchase a business. Dollar-for-dollar, the most accessible and cost effective business you can acquire is probably a network marketing business.

Network Marketing Overview

Network marketing is one of the fastest going areas for entrepreneurship available today. The relatively small start-up investment and the ability to leverage your time, money, activities, and knowledge make it probably the small business of choice for the 21st Century.

Although there are thousands of network marketing companies in the marketplace, there are three common-sense things to look for to increase your odds for success.

1. Look for a strong company—one with a solid financial position, experienced management, and a good track record.   Generally, companies that have been operating for three years or more with basically the same product and marketing plan are best.

2. Look for a product, goods or services, which everybody needs and relatively few people possess. For example, when NSA (National Safety Associates) started selling water filters, fewer than 3% of the homes in America had one. As concerns about water quality grew, sales increased to nearly 400 million dollars/year.

Also, products which are consumable and fulfill an important need such as weight loss or good nutrition are excellent for network marketing. They are consumed and repurchased on a regular basis.

3. Look for a company with a compensation plan that properly rewards you for your efforts. The plan should be simple and easy to understand and explain to others. Also, the initial investment required to get started should not be prohibitive. Plans which balance retail income, wholesale income, overrides, and bonuses, while rewarding you for training and duplication are generally most attractive.

Popular network marketing companies include:

• *Pre-Paid Legal Services, Inc.* This company understood that, in the most litigious country in the world, very few Americans had the time or resources to avail themselves of proper legal representation. As a result, this company is experiencing explosive growth.

• *Excel, ACN, and various long-distance telephone service providers.* These companies saw that, as a result of deregulation in the communications industry, they could provide something that nobody had and everybody needed, namely, low cost long-distance service. Their growth has accordingly been phenomenal.

• *Tom Danley's Tape of the Month.* This company tapped into the vast self-help and personal development market with monthly personal growth messages on audio tapes and CD's. With an affordable monthly subscription rate and a simple marketing plan, subscriber/associates can build a business with no inventory investment.

• **Amway.** One of the pioneers in Network Marketing. Amway gave distributors the opportunity to purchase household products at wholesale prices and sell them to others at retail, while receiving overrides and bonuses.

Other great companies may be found by getting information from the Direct Sellers Association and the Multi-Level Marketing International Association.

****

Once you have set up a wealth-building program, and commit to carry it out, you have basically solved the riddle of survival.

To properly benefit from the Universal Law of Value requires that your goals, your vision, and your purpose be clearly defined. They are the frame of reference on which you base your choices and make your decisions.

Chapter Summary

The Universal Law of Value and Mutual Exchange covers interactions between people on different levels of consciousness. This universal law states that you should not exchange the things that are important to you with people who are beneath your level of consciousness, or for things which are not worthy of your attention.

The guiding question from moment to moment is:

"What is the best use of my time, thoughts, energy, and resources, right now, in light of my goals. vision, and purpose?"

A primary application of the Universal Law of Value as applied to money is understood through the four principles of wealth. Network marketing is probably the small business choice for the 21st Century

Study Guide

1. Are you casting your pearls to swine? If so, why?

2. Are there situations where you have wasted your time and your money on other people?

3. Describe these situations and share how you will prevent them from reoccurring in the future.

Chapter IX

The Law
Of
Relationships

The Ninth Universal Law of Success is the Universal Law of Relationships. Every step of your success journey will involve relationships. Whether you are able to develop positive, gratifying, and empowering relationships to a large extent, determines whether and to what degree you will achieve your goals and realize your vision.

The Four Basic Relationships

There are four basic relationships.

1. Relationship with God.
2. Relationship with self.
3. Relationship with others.
4. Relationship with things.

When the relationships are proper, they are called harmonic relationships.

Harmonic relationships are relationships which are positive, encouraging, nurturing, and productive. They result in good health, happiness, love, success, prosperity, and positive, desired results. Harmonic relationships are based on truth, knowledge, understanding, faith, courage, self-confidence, and respect. When relationships are not harmonic, they are based on negative unproductive thoughts, habits, and feelings centered on ignorance, fear, doubt, dishonesty, and indecision.

Your Harmonic Relationship with God

Your harmonic relationship with God is expressed at Matthew 22:37-38:

*"Thou shalt love the Lord, thy God,
with all thy heart, and with all thy soul,
and with all thy mind.
This is the first and great commandment."*

In other words, the harmonic relationship between you and God is one of love. But then, ***"What is love?"***

Love is feeling, an emotion—a strong affection or attachment based on or arising out of kinship, admiration, benevolence, respect, compassion, tenderness, common interests, and generally positive emotions.

Metaphysically, heart is identified with your subconscious mind, soul is identified with your super-conscious mind, and mind relates to your conscious mind.

Thus, the harmonic relationship between you and God is one of total affection, attachment, respect, obedience, and feeling on every level of your being—your conscious, subconscious, and super-conscious minds. When this proper balance exists, you are in a harmonic relationship with God.

However, if you love God in your thoughts but do not express that love in your feelings, you are in disharmony. Even if you love God in your thoughts, express that love in your feelings, but have no faith in the power of God to manifest your vision, you are in disharmony. To achieve your goals and realize your vision, you must have a harmonic relationship with God. You must love God with all your heart, soul, and mind.

Your Harmonic Relationship with Yourself

How do you demonstrate your harmonic relationship with God?

You demonstrate your harmonic relationship with God by the way you love yourself—by the way you feel about yourself. Love and value must be internalized first, before they can be externalized to another person. We cannot give or share that which we do not first possess ourselves.

Your relationship with yourself is embodied in your self-image—how you feel about yourself. When your self-image is in tact, it is based on knowledge, love, courage, respect, faith, and confidence. You are then in a harmonic relationship with yourself.

Your Harmonic Relationship With Other People

The harmonic relationship between yourself and other people is described at Matthew 22:39:

"And the second (commandment) is like unto it,
Thou shalt love thy neighbor as thyself."

Another statement of the harmonic relationship between yourself and other people is:

". . . all things whatsoever ye would
that (people) should do to you,
do ye even so to them . . ."
—Matthew 7:12

In more familiar terms it may be stated as the Golden Rule:

"Do unto others,
as you would have them do unto you."

To love your neighbor as yourself implies that you must love—have a harmonic relationship with—yourself first, before you can love and have a harmonic relationship with another person. You demonstrate your love of self in the way you love other people.

Love requires self-esteem and independence. It is based on your ability to share yourself with others out of choice, and not out of dependent necessity. A harmonic relationship between two individuals is one in which both have the ability to sustain themselves separately.

True love, then, is a harmonic relationship between two people who each have a harmonic relationship with themselves. People who are dependent on each other remain in a relationship out of necessity or dependency, rather than choice. It is only when you are independent, when you have a harmonic relationship with yourself, that you are truly free to love another person and in turn have a harmonic relationship with them.

Nine Ways to Improve Your Relationships with Other People

1. Make yourself likable.

Your power to be liked by others is invaluable on your success journey. To be likable, you must first like yourself. Then this positive feeling you have about yourself will be projected to others through your attitude. When people like you, they will do things to help and assist you in accomplishing your goals and realizing your vision.

> *"A (person) who hath friends*
> *must show (themselves) friendly..."*
> —Proverbs 18:24

2. Always remember people's names.

There is no sound more pleasant to another person than the sound of his or her own name. When you remember people's names, they like it. It makes them feel that you think they are special.

3. Express appreciation for what other people do.

When you show appreciation for what others do, you give value to and validate their efforts.

4. Be lavish in your praise.

Praise expresses your approval of what others do. It uplifts them and inspires them to do even more.

5. Listen intently to other people's words, comprehending, understanding, and reacting to them.

Communication has too often become the practice

of two people, each waiting for the other person to finish talking so he or she can start talking again. Very few people really listen to the other person. They are too busy thinking about what they are going to say next. *How you listen is often more important than what you say.* Listen to the other person's whole story first before you formulate your response.

6. Let the interests of the other person be the topic of conversation.

The best way to get and keep another person's attention is not by smooth talk designed to impress them with your own accomplishments. You get their attention by encouraging them to talk about their own accomplishments, their goals, and aspirations.

7. Make the other person feel important.

Recognize and acknowledge the importance of everyone you meet. Always focus the conversation on the other person. Be conscious of their needs and do your best to meet those needs. Be courteous and helpful in ways that are meaningful to the other person.

8. Do not criticize.

Live above petty criticism. Treat others the way you would like to be treated. Let love motivate your attitudes and your actions. Desire the best for everyone you meet. Be willing to go the extra mile, especially if it will bring more knowledge and understanding.

When you throw dirt, you lose ground.

9. Always believe that there is a way to achieve the best results.

Know that people come into your life experience for

a reason. When your self-image is intact, be assured that you will only attract those people who are in harmony with how you feel about yourself. The others will be repelled by the positive aura that surrounds you.

Therefore, do not hold back in building positive relationships. Do all you can to nurture and develop these relationships into long term associations of positive, mutual benefit.

Words and Phrases Which Help You Develop Positive Relationships

The five most important words :
I am proud of you.

The four most important words:
What is your opinion?

The three most important words:
If you please.

The two most important words:
Thank you.

The single most important word:
Congratulations.

The least important word:
I

The highest and most powerful form of your relationship with other people is the formation of a Master Mind Group, and the practice of the Master Mind Principle.

The Master Mind Principle

"For where two or three are gathered in my name,
there I am in the midst of them."
               —Matthew 18:20

The Master Mind is the power source that creates, directs, and guides the universal creation. It is known by many names: God, First Cause, Supreme Being, Supreme Cause, Universal Force, and so on. Each of us, every person on the planet, is an individualized expression of this Master Mind. We have the God-given power to connect with and tap into the wisdom, creative genius, and power of this Master Mind.

As expressed in Genesis, God, the Universal Force, the Master Mind, is the creator of all things in existence. Genesis 1:27 provides:

"So God created man in his own image,
in the image of God created he him;
male and female created he them."

In order to tap into this power, a structured system of prayer has been developed to meet any challenge. It can be used to find the perfect solution to any problem confronting you. This system of prayer uses your own thoughts, strengths, and creative intelligence, together with the Infinite Intelligence of the Master Mind.

The mental energy of at least one other person is then added. The Master Mind Principle embodies the ancient concept that the combined energies, intelligence, and power of two or more like-minded people, is far greater than the sum total of their individual energy, intelligence, and power.

The Master Mind Principle is applied through a Master Mind Group.

A Master Mind Group consists of two or more persons who meet on a regular basis, in an atmosphere of trust and harmony. The purpose of the meeting is to provide mutual support and encouragement. It is not established for the purpose of solving each other's problems, but rather to turn problem areas, needs for healing, and any other good desires over to the Master Mind.

Meetings may be held in a home, place of business, restaurant, church—any mutually agreeable location. Meetings should be brief and held for the purpose intended. Meeting once a week is sufficient.

Conducting a Master Mind Meeting

A Master Mind meeting is conducted in the following manner:

One person acts as leader of the group and opens the meeting by reminding the group that there is a Master Mind, an infinite Presence and Power greater than themselves. This power is waiting to personally respond to them, if they only ask.

At the beginning of the meeting, a short period for sharing reports of progress, success, answered prayer, or goals achieved may be scheduled. This sharing helps establish a consciousness of excitement, success, and expectancy.

The leader then guides the group through the steps, one at a time. Each member verbally responds to each step, addressing the Master Mind in the presence of the group.

The Eight Steps of the Master Mind Process

1. I Surrender.

I admit that by myself, I am powerless to solve my own problems and improve my life. I need help.

2. I Believe.

I believe that a power greater than myself, the Master Mind, is responding to me in a very personal way.

3. I Understand.

I realize that erroneous, self-defeating thinking is the cause of my problems, failures, unhappiness, and fears.

4. I Decide.

I now decide to turn my life over to the Master Mind, surrendering my will and false beliefs.

5. I Forgive.

I forgive myself for all my mistakes. I also forgive and release everyone who has injured or harmed me in any way.

6. I Ask.

I now make my specific request to the Master Mind and my partners.

At this step, each member of the Master Mind group states their prayer needs and receives the support of the other members of the group. After each prayer request, the other members of the group affirm together:

"I know that the Master Mind has heard you. You will receive and experience that which you have asked for and more."

7. I Gratefully Accept.

I gratefully accept and give thanks, knowing that the miracle-working power of the Master Mind has responded to my every request and need.

I acknowledge and assume the feelings I would have as if my requests were already granted.

8. Dedication and Covenant.

I now make a covenant which provides that the Master Mind will supply me with all things necessary to live a success-filled and happy life.

I dedicate myself to be of continuous service to God and my fellow man, to live my life as a positive example for others to follow. I remain an open channel for God's will and direction.

I go forth with a spirit of love, enthusiasm, and expectancy.

I am at peace with myself.

Your Harmonic Relationship with Things

"Lay not up for yourselves treasures upon earth,
where moth and rust doth corrupt,
and where thieves break through and steal,
But lay up for yourselves treasures in heaven,
where neither moth nor rust doth corrupt,
and where thieves do not break through nor steal;
For where your treasure is,
there will your heart be also."
—Matthew 6: 19, 20-21

Remember that you are the master of the planet, given power and dominion over all things therein. Your treasure is that which is important to you; that which you value deeply; that which you hold strong feelings for in your heart, in your subconscious mind.

When you place your values and deep inner feelings in material possessions or things outside yourself, which can be stolen or destroyed, you relinquish your God-given power. If you place your values in these material possessions, they will rule and control you.

Some may argue that you can have a harmonic relationship with God and love material possessions at the same time. But, this contradiction is covered at Matthew 6:24:

> *"No (person) can serve two masters;*
> *for either (they) will hate the one,*
> *and love the other:*
> *or else (they) will hold to one,*
> *and despise the other.*
> *Ye cannot serve God and mammon*
> *(material possessions)."*

Therefore, put your values and deep inner feelings in heaven—thoughts and consciousness—and not in things, material possessions. The harmonic relationship between you and things is one in which material possessions serve you, and are for your benefit and enjoyment. Your may enjoy material possessions, they must neither rule nor control you.

The harmonic relationship between you and things is set forth in Matthew 6:31-33:

> *"Therefore, take no thought (do not worry) saying,*
> *What shall we eat? or, What shall we drink? or,*
> *Wherewithal shall we be clothed? . . .*
> *But seek ye first the kingdom of God,*
> *and (its) righteousness;*
> *and all these things shall be added unto you."*

When you develop a harmonic relationship with God, and follow the dictates of that relationship, you have a guide for establishing a harmonic relationship with yourself, others, and things. Follow that guide and everything you need will come to you. The thoughts, the people, and the material necessities required to achieve your goals and realize your vision and purpose will be yours for the asking.

Chapter Summary

The Universal Law of Relationships covers the nature or character of your personal contacts and interactions. The four basic relationships are with God, yourself, other people, and things. When these relationships are positive, they are harmonic. When they are negative, they are disharmonic. Relationships may be established, developed, and improved. The nine ways to improve your relationships with other people can help build positive, long-term associations of mutual benefit.

The Master Mind Principle describes a relationship between a group of two or more people centered on God—the Master Mind. Applying this principle, the combined energies, intelligence, and power of the group, is far greater than the sum total of their individual energies.

Study Guide

1. Which of the four basic relationships do you need to work on? Why?

2. Choose one of the nine ways to improve your relationship with other people to focus on each week. Practice and implement it in your daily activities.

Chapter X

The Law
Of
Supply

The Tenth Universal Law of Success is the Universal Law of Supply And Opportunity. Everything necessary for abundant life is ever-present and always available. Opportunity is infinite. There is an endless supply of whatever you need, wherever you are.

"Take no thought, saying
What shall we eat? or,
What shall we drink? or,
Wherewhithal shall we be clothe?
. . . for your heavenly Father knoweth
that ye have need of all these things.
But seek ye first the kingdom of God,
and his righteousness;
and all these things shall be added unto you."
—Matthew 6:31-33

Where is the kingdom of God?

Is it someplace over there, beyond the clouds? Is it on the other side of life? No, the answer is given in Luke 17: 20,21:

"the kingdom of God cometh not with observation.
Neither shall they say, Lo here! or, lo there!
For, behold, the kingdom of God is within you."

What is the kingdom of God?

"For the kingdom of God
is not meat and drink;,
But righteousness, and peace, and joy
in the Holy Ghost."
—Romans 14:17

It is not the physical, sensual, or material things that embody the kingdom of God. The kingdom of God is a condition of the mind. It is a state of consciousness in which the mind, body, and soul are in harmony with the Divine Mind. Specifically, it is that state of consciousness in which your conscious, subconscious, and super-conscious minds are in harmony with the God Mind.

The kingdom of God also represents a projection of Divine Ideas, the universal rhythms, into your own mind. Thus, the kingdom of God is the kingdom of thoughts and ideas. On a practical level, the Universal Law of Supply states that you should seek thoughts and ideas first.

To obtain the health, wealth, and happiness you desire, look first within yourself for thoughts and ideas which are in harmony with health, wealth, and happiness. Then, to actually make these thoughts and ideas manifest in your life experience, you must do more than just think about them. You must take action. You must *SEEK* the kingdom. Pursue these thoughts and ideas actively, intelligently, and continuously. Know that you will experience health, wealth, and happiness as a result of your efforts.

Do not worry, fear, or doubt. Keep your thoughts centered on the vision in your mind that you wish to realize in your life. Believe in that vision. Have faith in your own ability to do whatever it takes to realize that vision.

Understand that the Universal Law of Supply guarantees that there is no lack or limitation in God, Divine Mind. ***There is always an endless supply of whatever you need, to get whatever you want.*** Scarcity, lack, and limitation exist only in your mind. Since you control the thoughts that fill your mind, you can do anything you want to do, have anything you want to have, and be whatever you want to be.

If you think abundance in your thoughts, see abundance in your imagination—your mind's eye, feel abundance in your heart, and believe abundance in your soul, you will have abundance in your life experience.

> *"Blessed (are those) who walketh not*
> *in the counsel of the ungodly,*
> *nor standeth in the way of sinners,*
> *nor sitteth in the seat of the scornful.*
> *But (their) delight is in the law of the Lord;*
> *and in (God's) law*
> *do (they) meditate day and night.*
> *. . .and whatsoever (they) doeth shall prosper."*
> —Psalm 1:1-3

Putting it simply, when you are in harmony with the Universal Laws of Success, whatever you try works, whatever you need appears.

Where there is unlimited supply,
there are unlimited opportunities.

Opportunity Is Always Right Where You Are!

Opportunity is a favorable combination of circumstances in a particular endeavor; a good chance or occasion to advance yourself. It is derived from the word *opportune* which means right for the purpose; fitting in regard to circumstances; well timed; happening or done at the right time.The word *opportune* comes from the Latin *opportunus* which means at or before the port; at the door.

An opportunity, then, is a circumstance or series of circumstances which place you at the door—the door to success, the door to abundance, the door to infinite possibilities for health, wealth, happiness, love, reward, and growth. *How do you come to stand before this door of opportunity?*

Realize that the law of supply is always operating. The source of the health, wealth, and happiness that you desire is inside your mind. Therefore, **you stand before the door to opportunity as a result of your own thoughts.**

If you permit yourself to be a negative thinker, then your thoughts are of lack, limitation, failure, and fear. You will not see the door to opportunity. In fact, a series of circumstances which could greatly benefit you could present themselves and you would not even see them.

You would be so involved with what you do not have, what you can not do, and what you cannot become, that you would be unaware that the opportunity has presented itself, and the door is right where you are.

The negative thinker would see that door to opportunity as an impassable obstacle, and turn away convinced that *"it can't be done!"* or, *"they don't have what it takes."* As, one by one, the opportunities in life are rejected or ignored, the negative thinker goes deeper and deeper into a created reality of lack, limitation, failure, fear, and poverty.

The noted English surgeon, Thomas Jones (1810-1880), described this experience, saying:

> *"Many do with opportunities*
> *as children do at the seashore,*
> *they fill their little hands with sand,*
> *and let the grains fall through,*
> *one by one, till all are gone."*

When you are a positive, possibility thinker, the Universal Law of Supply goes immediately to work for you. That which you are seeking, is seeking you; that which you ask for, is rushing to be granted; and wherever you knock, it begins to open for you. Put simply, *"What you see is what you get!"*

When you are a positive thinker, you see those same circumstances as a door to great opportunity for the health, wealth, happiness, and success you are seeking. Believing in your own abilities, you will open that door, enter, and receive your blessings.

There is never a lack of opportunity. Opportunity, like supply, is infinite and ever present. How you perceive an opportunity, however, depends on your level of consciousness. If you have a low level of consciousness, centered on things—the material world of facts and appearances—then your perception of an opportunity is limited by those same facts and circumstances.

For example, many people think that a college degree is essential for success. Based on that belief, they then feel that they cannot be successful until they get their college degree. So, when certain circumstances—opportunities for advancement in their profession—present themselves, they do not see them as opportunities. They have accepted the limitation of not having a college degree, as an insurmountable obstacle. Thus, they will not permit themselves to take advantage of the opportunities that exist, right where they are.

On the other hand, a person of a higher level of consciousness, centered on God and spiritual principles, with or without a college degree, would see those same circumstances as great opportunities for completion, success, happiness, and wealth. On the higher level of consciousness, *"all things are possible."*

". . . with God all things are possible."
—Matthew 19:26

Every circumstance you experience in life is an opportunity for completion and growth. Whether they be positive experiences of joy and happiness, or negative experiences of suffering and despair, the potential for growth, reward, and benefit is an ever-present opportunity.

Chapter Summary

The Universal Law of Supply and Opportunity provides that everything you need in life is always available. There is an endless supply of whatever you need, wherever you are, to get whatever you want. Opportunity is a favorable combination of circumstances in a particular endeavor. It is the right and proper door to be opened to receive the objects of your desires. However, you stand before this door as a result of your own thoughts.

Study Guide

1. Have you passed up opportunities in the past?

2. What were they?

3. What were your thoughts when you let the opportunity pass without taking action?

Chapter XI

The Law
Of
Persistence

The Eleventh Universal Law of Success is the Universal Law of Persistence and Results. Simply stated it provides: If you persist in doing the right things, you will get the right results. Biblically, the Universal Law of Persistence and Results is:

". . . Ask, and it shall be given you;
Seek, and ye shall find;
Knock, and it shall be opened unto you."

"For everyone that asked, receiveth;
And (they) that seeketh, findeth;
And to (them) that knocketh, it shall be opened."
—Luke 11: 9,10

When you persist in your efforts to achieve a desired result, you are asking the Universal Mind—the God Mind—to grant you that desired result in your life experience.

Persistence is the one trait that virtually all successful people have in common. It is the sustained effort you must acquire to induce faith in your own ability to get the desired results in your endeavors. Your persistence is a measure of your faith in your own abilities and skills. The more persistent you are about achieving a particular outcome, the greater your belief in yourself and your abilities.

Without persistence, you will not be successful.

Each of us is endowed with the power of persistence. Sometimes we use this power in the wrong direction, about the wrong things. Some people are more persistent in pursuing failure than pursuing success.

Persistence must always be combined with intelligence. The age-old saying, *"If at first you don't succeed, then try and try again,"* must be clarified by adding the thought: *try again in different and better ways.* Do not get bogged down being persistent in using wrong methods. It is much more rewarding to be persistent in finding new and better methods to get your desired results.

When the going gets tough, the tough get going.

When you are persistent in your efforts, the law of averages works in your favor. The harmonic universe is filled with positive experiences and negative experiences. When you persist through the negative experiences, and keep right on going—no matter what— then it is you who is in place when the positive experiences begin to flow. In fact, it is the faith generated by your persistence that attracts the positive experiences in the first place.

> **When you get to the end of your rope,
> tie a knot in it and hang on.**

I AM.   I WILL.

Persistence is the expression of your will to win, to overcome, to survive, to complete whatever you set out to do. Your will is the moment-to-moment expression of your ego—your awareness of your self-concept. It is that intangible yet real force which expresses itself as the *"I"* in you. Your ego, or *"I"* manifests on two levels.

First, your ego is expressed as *"I AM"*, that you exist, you are real. Then, as *"I WILL,"* which expresses your desire and determination to act. The *"I WILL"* is the expression of the Life Force within you.

> *Your WILL gives you the power to persist when all indications and appearances say you cannot win.*

> *"When you get into a tight place and everything goes against you, until it seems that you cannot hold on a minute longer, never give up then; for that is just the place and time that the tide will turn."*
> —Harriet Beecher Stowe

> *"Man is made great or little by his own will."*
> —Johann Schiller

Why do people give up, let go, or quit?
People give up and quit because they do not have the

WILL to win. They have no faith in themselves, no faith in God, and no faith in their own abilities. They become discouraged and quit at the appearance of adversity or when they encounter bumps in the road to success.

It may not be the first adversity or the first bump in the road. But sooner or later, if the *WILL* is weak, they give up and accept defeat—usually, one step away from victory.

> *"Persistent people begin their success*
> *where others end in failure."*
> —Edward Eggleston

> **A winner never quits,**
> **and a quitter never wins.**

Adverse conditions should motivate you to try even harder and smarter. See yourself bigger than the things which try to stop you; stronger than the obstacles which confront you; using the stumbling blocks placed in your path as stepping stones to greater and greater opportunities for victory, success, and personal completion.

> *"Victory belongs to the most persevering."*
> —Napoleon

It is the struggle to get free from the things that hinder or bind you; to overcome the obstacles in your way; to rise above the appearances of defeat and failure, that develops the faith and the power to find a way when there is no way, to do that which seems impossible.

> **Without struggle, there is no growth.**
> **Without growth, there is no victory.**

"The virtue lies in the struggle, not in the prize."
—Richard Milnes

Obstacles To Persistence

The main obstacles to the habit of persistence are the fear of criticism, the fear of failure, and the habit of procrastination.

The fear of criticism takes away your drive, your creativity, and your self-confidence. If you permit yourself to hear criticism, it can make you doubt yourself, become indecisive, and discouraged. Realize that most people criticize others out of ignorance, envy, jealousy, and feelings of inferiority. As long as you are being criticized, you are probably doing the right things to succeed.

The fear of failure takes the wind out of your sails. It is manifestation of a lack of faith in yourself and in your abilities. In essence, this fear is a lack of faith in God. To overcome the fear of failure, realize that to fail means you are trying. The more you fail, the more you find new ways to try again. You literally fail your way to success, if you just do not quit.

The habit of procrastination is the number-one cause of failure. For example, you can recognize the value of persistence, but procrastinate in getting started practicing persistence. Everything that happens in the world is being done now, in the present. The only time to take action on your goals and vision is now. Whatever happens tomorrow is already determined by what you did or did not do today.

If you procrastinate and put off until tomorrow what

should have been done today, then you have already determined tomorrow, which could only have been changed today.

Procrastination is the thief of time. Persistence is built through continuous action. Procrastination is built through continuous inaction. Where there is no purposeful action, through procrastination or otherwise, there can be no persistence, and thus no success.

You strengthen the habit of procrastinating when you put off making decisions until it is time to take action; fail to keep track of your time; and postpone unpleasant tasks until you are in a crisis or critical situation.

How To Overcome Procrastination

1. Realize that procrastination is one of the main causes of failure.

2. Realize that when you permit procrastination to operate in your life:
   a. You waste time.
   b. Your duties go unperformed.
   c. You miss opportunities.
   d. You miss important engagements.
   e. Your life slips away like grains of sand in the wind, until there is nothing left.

3. Have a definite schedule and stick to it. Schedule your routine duties.

4. Make a list of the things you have to do, or want to do, other than your routine activities. Set a definite time to review this list, and decide which items you are going to do and which ones you will not do. Forget the ones you decide not to do. Schedule a definite time to do each of the remaining items.

5. Make a definite commitment to always be on time for all engagements. Have an accurate watch and look at it often.

6. Make realistic assessments of the amount of time required for each activity/item, and allow yourself enough time to make adequate preparations so that you will be properly prepared.

7. Plan to handle one activity/item at a time until it is completed.

8. When you are confronted with complex or extensive activity/items, analyze them completely. Break them down into smaller activity/items and handle each of them one at a time.

9. Be careful not to crowd your calendar with so many appointments that it is virtually impossible to make them all on time with proper preparations.

10. Do not let fear of criticism or fear of failure cause you to be slow in making decisions. Decide intelligently, act effectively, and **do it now!**

Overcome procrastination to get started.
Ignore criticism to keep going.

Persistence is a success habit which you can develop and perfect through consistent practice.

Eight Ways to Develop
the Habit of Persistence

1. Have a clearly defined, internalized vision of your purpose, and a burning, deep desire for its realization. This is the fire which feeds your *WILL* to act. If it is not clearly defined and internalized through your senses, you cannot generate the personal power needed to hang tough and keep moving, no matter what.

2. Analyze your vision and break it down into specific goals. These goals become the targets on which you focus the power of your *WILL*.

3. Have a definite plan expressed in continuous action to achieve each of your goals. These are the step-by-step activity/items that you handle on a daily basis. Do not stop too soon for rest, reward, holidays, birthdays, and so on.

4. Have a friendly alliance with one or more people who encourage you to follow through with your plans or purpose. Form a Master Mind alliance. This is a group of two or more people, sharing knowledge and effort in a spirit of harmony for the attainment of a desired result.

5. Decide once and for all that failure is just a temporary pause, not a destination.
To fail proves that you are trying. Each failure has a lesson to be learned. *You literally fail your way to success.*

It's not how many times you stumble down.
It's the number of times
you pick yourself up off the ground.
And keep moving on to meet your goals.

6. Realize that *"something for nothing"* **is an illusion.** Everything of value requires that you put forth effort to obtain it. Remember, the only place that success comes before work is in the dictionary.

7. Stop wishing your life away. Start doing what must be done to achieve your desired results—your goals. Change your wishbone to a backbone. Have faith in yourself, in your God, and in your vision and purpose. It has been said, *"It's not the size of the dog in the fight that counts, so much as the size of the fight in the dog."* It's the *size of the fight* in you that really matters as you strive to reach your goals, realize your vision, and achieve your purpose.

8. Do It Now. Take Immediate Action. All that is being done is being done now. Nothing has ever happened tomorrow. All that truly matters is decided by the action you take right now.

Practice persistence in all you do.
Desired results will come to you.

Chapter Summary

The Universal Law of Persistence provides that if you persist in doing the right things, you will get the right results. Persistence is the sustained effort you must acquire to induce faith in your own ability to get the desired results in whatever you do. Without persistence, you will not be successful. The main obstacles to persistence are fear and procrastination. Procrastination is a learned habit which must be overcome. Persistence is a learned skill which should be developed and perfected.

Study Guide

1. Think of situations which, had you persisted, would have turned out differently. Write them down.

2. What made you give up and quit in each situation?

3. How could you have done things differently?

4. If procrastination has been one of your challenges, what are you doing right now to overcome this habit?

Chapter XII

The Law
Of
Truth

The Twelfth Universal Law of Success is the Universal Law of Truth.

*"And ye shall know the truth,
and the truth shall make you free."*
—John 8:32

And what is this truth that makes you free. The truth that makes you free is your basic understanding of the universe, the laws and principles by which it operates, and how you fit in to that universe. Truth is the foundation of the universe.

*"Therefore, whosoever hearth these sayings . . .
and doeth them,*

I will liken (them) unto a wise (person,)
who built (their) house upon a rock.
And the rain descended, and the floods came,
and the winds blew and beat upon that house,
and it fell not; for it was founded upon a rock."
—Matthew 7:24-25

The Nine Elements of Truth

1. There is a First Cause. Whether we call it God, Universal Force, Divine Mind, The Creator, or by any other name, it is the same First Cause. Call it The Creator.

2. This Creator has an intelligence which operates through order and principle.

3. This intelligence through order and principle is all powerful, all knowing, and everywhere at once.

4. This intelligence operating through order and principle is the power of truth, which is whole and complete, encompassing the positive and the negative of all things— the good, the bad, life and death.

5. Everything created in the universe embodies this power of truth, through intelligence, order and principle, in accord with its nature.

6. Humankind was created in the nature and image of The Creator, and endowed with certain inalienable rights and powers by this Creator.

7. These rights and powers of humankind are maximized when they are congruent and harmonic with the power of truth as established by The Creator.

8. The Universal Laws of Success are an integral part of the power of truth which guides humankind to a harmonic relationship with the universe and the Creator.

9. When these elements of truth are studied, practiced, internalized, and mastered, you will know the truth and you will be free.

Mastering The Power of Truth

Master the Twelve Universal Laws of Success to guide you on your journey to your goals, vision, and purpose. Digest and understand these laws as simple, concise statements of truth which you can quickly and automatically articulate in your consciousness.

The following is a concise statement of the Twelve Universal Laws of Success:

1. The Universal Law of Thought
You become what you think about most of the time.

What you recognize, you energize. What you energize, you realize.

2. The Universal Law of Change.
You change your life by changing your thinking.

3. The Universal Law of Vision.
What you see clearly in your thoughts is what you get in your life experience.

4. The Universal Law of Command.
What you say is what you get.

5. The Universal Law of Human Magnetism.
Like attracts Like. Be the person you want to be to attract the people you want to meet, the experiences you wish to have, and the possessions you seek to enjoy.

"What you wear in your heart,
comes out in your face."
—Lavinia E. Sneed

6. The Universal Law of Focus and Discipline.

Keep your eye on the prize. All distractions are equal and equally counter-productive. Keep yourself under control at all times.

7. The Universal Law of Action.

How to be most effective in doing what must be done.

8. The Universal Law of Value and Mutual Exchange.

Invest your time, thoughts, energies, and money wisely and effectively. There is no such thing as a free lunch.

"If your outflow exceeds your income,
your upkeep becomes your downfall"
—Russell Hemphill

9. The Universal Law of Relationships.

Do unto others as you would have them do unto you.

"If you want to have friends, be friendly."
—Elder Linwood Nesbitt

10. The Universal Law of Supply and Opportunity.

There is always enough of just what you need.

11. The Universal Law of Persistence and Results.

A winner never quits, and a quitter never wins. Hang tough and keep rolling.

l2. The Law of Truth.
The truth shall make you free.

Truth Principles

Integrated with these Universal Laws of Success are other truth principles which effect all aspects of your thoughts, emotions, and actions.

These principles are:

1. The principle of perfection.

"Be ye, therefore, perfect,
even as your Father,
which is in heaven, is perfect."
—Matthew 5:48

Be the highest and best that you can be. It is your nature to seek the good and the positive in all situations, circumstances, and associations.

Your Father—your source—is in consciousness, which is whole, complete, and perfect. Establishing a harmonic relationship with your source puts you on the right path in all things.

2. The principle of prayer.

There must be a daily, personal communication with your Creator. This communication should be a prayer of alignment, which puts you in rhythm and harmony with all that is good for you.

"Blessed is the (person)
who walketh not in the counsel of the ungodly,

nor standeth in the way of sinners,
nor sitteth in the seat of the scornful.
But (their) delight is in the law of the Lord;
and in (this) law do (they) meditate day and night."
—Psalms 1:1,2

Good fortune comes to you when you stay away from negative people, thoughts, and activities. Avoid those who have already messed up their lives, and who have no respect for God, themselves, or others.

Focus your life on the law of truth at all times.

The Lord's Prayer makes it perfectly clear:

"Give us this day our daily bread."
—Matthew 6:11

3. The principle of forgiveness.

"For if ye forgive (people) their trespasses,
your heavenly Father will also forgive you;
But if ye forgive not (people) their trespasses,
neither will your Father forgive your trespasses."
—Matthew 6:14,15

You must forgive and release other people for what they do or have done to you. This protects you from the negative emotions of jealousy, envy, revenge, and blame. Also, forgive and release yourself for what you have done to yourself. This frees you from the negative emotions of insecurity, self-sabotage, and guilt.

4. The principle of motive.

Your motive is the intelligence identified with the deepest feelings associated with your thoughts. They are the subconscious aspect of each conscious thought.

> *". . . thy Father, who is in secret;*
> *and thy Father, who seeth in secret,*
> *shall reward thee openly."*
>
> —Matthew 6:6

The Father, the Force, the Creator manifests that which is in your deepest feelings into your life experience. The motive of another person is transmitted through their subconscious mind, directly to your subconscious mind. You perceive their motive through your intuition, your sixth sense. Trust your intuition. It is not what a person says or does, but rather the feelings associated with their motives that determines how that person will interact with you. You may hide the appearance of your motive, but you cannot hide its effects.

5. The principle of right judgment.

> *"Judge not, that ye be not judged.*
> *For what judgment ye judge, ye shall be judged;*
> *and with what measure ye mete (measure),*
> *it shall be measured to you again."*
>
> —Matthew 7:1-2

> *"Thou hypocrite,*
> *first cast out the beam out of thine own eye,*
> *and then shalt thou see clearly*
> *to cast out the mote out of thy brother's eye."*
>
> —Mathew 7:5

To judge is to form an opinion about something or someone after careful inquiry and evaluation. The principle of judgment provides that you must be righteous and fair in your inquiries and evaluation of other people. Make righteous judgments at all times, and in all circumstances. If you are unfair, prejudiced, and biased in forming opinions about others, you will create a negative, hostile response of hatred and revenge. This negative response is directed back at you.

If you judge another person righteously, then you demonstrate a positive attitude which creates an atmosphere of truth, fairness, and respect. That which you radiate and project by righteous judgment, you attract and receive in the judgments of other people about you.

6. The principle of discernment.

Be not deceived by appearances. To be successful, you must learn to see the truth in every circumstance and situation. You must become a quick and accurate judge of people and their motives.

> *"Beware of false prophets,*
> *which come to you in sheep's clothing,*
> *but inwardly they are ravening wolves."*
> *Ye shall know them by their fruits . . ."*
> *Even so, every good tree*
> *bringeth forth good fruit,*
> *but a corrupt tree bringeth forth evil fruit.*
> *A good tree cannot bring forth evil fruit,*
> *neither can a corrupt tree bring forth good fruit."*
>
> *"Wherefore, by their fruits ye shall know them."*
> —Matthew 7:15-18, 20

Rely on your own intuition, common sense, and understanding of the laws and principles of success to discern the truth in any situation.

Life leaves clues of principle and experience.

Be totally observant and sensitive to your inner voice and feelings.

The Law of Cause and Effect

The source of your power of discernment is your understanding of the Universal Law of Cause and Effect. The universe operates by order and principle manifesting through cause and effect. When you align yourself with this order and these principles, the operation of cause and effect reveals the truth in all things.

****

The Universal Law of Truth is internalized through faith and feeling that there is always a right and positive solution. It guarantees that you already have everything you need to get everything you want, to go wherever you want to go, and to become the person you want to become.

Chapter Summary

The Law of Truth is the foundation on which you build your life. Mastering the universal laws of success will guide you on your success journey to your goals, vision, and purpose. Integrated into the success laws are truth principles which facilitate interpretation and implementation.

Study Guide

1. Which of the universal laws do you need to focus on first?

2. What is your plan of attack?

Epilogue

Today
Is
Yesterday's
Tomorrow

Today Is Tomorrow's Yesterday!

Today is the actual result of the effectiveness of your plans. If you fully utilized each and every hour available yesterday, then you have done all you can to maximize your possibilities for achievement, reward, and success today. If you wasted those precious moments of yesterday in frivolous, unproductive endeavors, your rewards will come in like fashion today. Along with the results of your previous efforts, today also contains the seeds of tomorrow's possibilities.

Today embraces the opportunity to make tomorrow the way you want it to be. Today is your last chance to influence and change the results that will surely come forth tomorrow. Each day represents the results and proof of your previous endeavors, together with an opportunity for change in the future.

Seize upon this daily opportunity for change with a positive attitude and a definite plan. Put this plan into immediate action through continuous, effective work. The results of your efforts today will surely appear as tomorrow's reality. Where you are tomorrow depends on how wisely and effectively you use the hours available today.

Start each day with a positive mental attitude. Visualize and focus on your goals. Carefully make your plans. Write them down in detail. List the things that must be done each day to accomplish your goals. Use every hour of every day to execute your plans effectively to produce desired results. At the end of each day, ask yourself the daily question:

Did I do everything I could today to make tomorrow the way I want it to be?

When you can answer the daily question in the absolute affirmative:

Yes, I did everything I could, with all I had to do it with!

you are well on your way to the success and achievement you seek and deserve in this lifetime.

"Come to the cliff," He said.
"We are afraid," they said.
"Come to the cliff," He said
They came. He pushed them,
And they flew.

—Amir Solomon

About The Author

Herbert Harris entered Columbia University after his junior year of high school. He received a special scholarship to attend Columbia without first completing high school.

Graduating from Columbia University with a BA degree, majoring in physics, Mr. Harris did research in theoretical and high energy physics.

Leaving the scientific arena, Herbert worked at Time Magazine in New York City before launching a free lance writing career that eventually evolved into a nationally syndicated newspaper column called **Thoughts For Success.** This column is syndicated to over 200 newspapers.

A collection of these newspaper articles were assembled into a book called **Power Thoughts For Your Success.**

Mr. Harris teamed up with Lucien Farrar to write **How To Make Money In Music**, a highly popular guide book to the music industry, published by Arco/ Prentice Hall.

Herbert Harris took advantage of the New York State Clerkship Law to become a lawyer without attending law school. Under the tutelage of distinguished New York attorney Benjamin Sneed, Harris taught himself law and passed the New York State Bar Examination. Herbert is probably the last person to be admitted to practice law in the State of New York without ever attending law school.

After operating his law firm for many years, Mr. Harris retired from his law practice to pursue a full-time writing and lecturing career.

Herbert has forever been a student, actively pursuing his religious, esoteric, philosophical, and metaphysical studies in Africa, Israel, Egypt, and wherever else he had to go.

His latest book, *The Twelve Universal Laws of Success* provides an organized, straight forward, step-by-step approach to basic success principles and the laws under which they operate. This book has attracted worldwide attention and has been translated into many languages including Chinese, Italian, Portugese, and Spanish.

Mr. Harris has done numerous seminars, workshops, and lectures at churches, universities and corporations throughout the country, including: First Church of Religious science, University of North Carolina, Ohio State University, African Methodist Episcopal Church, Lucent Technology, Small Business Technology Development Centers, Chambers of Commerce, and National Safety Associates.

Harris also developed Achievement Motivation, an interactive personal skills development course designed to reduce the dropout rate among college students.

Mr. Harris is personal coach, sales trainer and Master Facilitator. He is co-founder, organizer, and Master Facilitator of the *Community Action Group*, a citizens advocacy group that was named Community Organization of the Year by the Human Relations Commission.

Herbert also heads Connections Unlimited, a political and marketing consulting firm that successfully handled city, county and state political campaigns.

Mr. Harris, in high demand as a consultant, speaker, and facilitator, divides his time between writing, speaking, and conducting LifeSkills® Seminars/ Workshops.

LifeSkill® Seminars and Workshops

LifeSkill® seminars and workshops are designed to be exciting, informative and interactive. Each seminar follows a *workbook* to be completed as the seminar progresses. This involvement increases retention.

* * * * * * * * * * * * *

Leadership Seminar

Introduce basic leadership principles in a format that stimulates active participation. The collaborative team approach is explored and developed.

Time Management Seminar

Covers the fundamental principles of time management with practical exercises designed to immediately increase daily effectiveness.

The Twelve Universal Laws of Success

Personal development seminar that incorporates spiritual principles into a practical self-help action approach to success. Topics include: improving self-esteem, overcoming obstacles, fear and worry; building self-discipline; making success plans; wealth building; improving relationships; overcoming procrastination

LifeSkill® Workshop for Parents

Interactive personal skills development workshop that focuses on empowering parents to be more proactive in the education of their children

Motivational Speeches and Lectures

Brief motivational talks, 20 to 60 minutes, that inspire listeners to strive for personal excellence in their jobs, professions and personal lives. Appropriate for churches, businesses, schools, conventions, sales meetings etc. Our *"Flying with the Eagles"* and *"This time it's You"* presentations are especially popular.

The LifeSkill® Institute, Inc.
P.O. Box 302
Wilmington, NC 28402
(800) 570-4009

I am interested in learning more about The LifeSkill® Institute, Inc. Please send me the FREE Success Questionnaire. (**The Success Questionnaire is a personal diagnostic of your strengths, and the areas you need to work on. It helps resolve the issues that have blocked, or diminished you prospects for success.**)

My name is_____

Address_____

City/State/Zip_____

Telephone #: (Home)_____(Bus)_____

I would like information about:

a._____Becoming an Associate of the LifeSkill® Institute, Inc.

b._____Leadership Seminars

c._____Time Management Seminars

d._____Twelve Universal Laws of Success Seminars

e._____LifeSkill® Workshops for Parents

f._____Motivational Speeches and Lectures

g._____Audio & Video tapes.

I would like to order_____copies of this book

@ $14.95/bk.— — — — — — — — —   _____

Sales Tax: NC residents (only) add 7%   _____

Shipping: Add $3.00 per book.   _____

Total Amount Enclosed (ck/mo)   _____

Make check payable to LifeSkill® Institute, Inc.

Make a copy of this page, fill it out, and send it to the above address.

Notes

BookWire Review: December 2004

"This book is sure to find the approval of every one who reads it, and is going to find its place amongst classic self-help books. Herbert Harris will with this book be a household name in the manner of Dale Carnegie and Napoleon Hill."

Barnesandnoble.com Reviews:

Michael O, a Sales Instructor from Chicago:

Great book *"This by far is one of the most inspiring motivational books I have ever read. I read it from cover to cover and did not want to put it down. The questions from the study guide at the end of each chapter really helped you to reinforce the material. I am going to tell everyone I know about this book. It is awesome."*

John Hughes, reviewer:

"This book is as 5 Star find that should be added to everyone's collection of motivational treasures. The author uses spiritual references that relate to each success principal he discusses. ... I would recommend it to anyone looking to make positive changes in their lives. It is especially useful for parents with children who are making critical decisions about their future education and careers. The summaries at the end of each chapter make this book a hands-on resource for achieving one's life goals."

Amazon.com Reviews

Joanna Daneman (Middletown, DE USA)

"The 12 Laws of Success are nothing new to those of you who read inspirational material such as Napoleon Hill or Dr. Robert Schuller. That's ok, because this 196-page yellow-covered volume is very excellent summary and reference. The bright school-bus yellow cover is easily visible on the shelf--

ready to grab when you need a word of advice.

I like this book for the concise writing and excellent summary of the laws. I recommend it as a gift to graduating students, anyone starting out looking for work, anyone just in a new job, or even just someone who needs a boost. It should be on every family's bookshelf and I don't say that casually. This is the kind of information that can work its way deep into your lifetime habits and make a real difference. Highly recommended for just about anyone."

Donald Mitchell, reviewer, author and consultant

The Twelve Universal Laws of Success is not explicitly derived from Napoleon Hill's popular works . . . but it is clearly an intellectual heir of that work. If you liked Mr. Hill's work, you will probably enjoy this book very much. If you do not know Mr. Hill's work, you could do worse than to begin with this book instead of Mr. Hill's books.

Although almost everyone admires Napoleon Hill's work on the requirements for being successful, most will agree that he was always somewhat opaque in describing what he had learned. His later books are clearer, but not crystal clear. For that reason, I'm always pleased when someone connects the dots better on the same subject.

The Twelve Universal Laws of Success is such a book. I am very glad I read it. Mr. Herbert Harris does quite a remarkable job of combining the perspectives of physical science, psychology and different religions to provide a very clear view of how to lead a life directed towards worthy goals that you achieve. Those who are Christians will find strength in his use of many Biblical quotations.

As I read the twelve laws, I sometimes felt like I was being taken on a tour around a statue. By seeing more perspectives, I could understand the holism of the statue much better . . . or in this case, what is required for success. So don't be surprised at what will seem like a little redundancy in the rules. Some of them are really axioms of other rules . . . but ones that you might not have figured out on your own. For example, the law of change is an axiom of the law of thought.

The material is well organized. The book begins with much helpful background information, including how to study any new subject or book. Now, that's getting down to brass tacks! Each law then has its own chapter, and you will find chapter summaries and study guides at the end of each. If you apply yourself to the study guides, your benefit from the book will be enormous. That's one of the many improvements over Napoleon Hill in the book.

I also liked the way that Mr. Harris was careful to explain what his words and concepts mean. Success is 'the continuous realization of the outcomes or results you desire.' He also carefully describes the conscious, subconscious and superconscious minds.

The laws themselves are ones that most people will recognize from their own experiences and religious studies.

I especially liked his advice for how to end your day. Ask yourself, 'Did I do everything I could do today to make tomorrow the way I want it to be?' He encourages you to live each day so that you can earnestly answer, 'Yes, I did everything I could, with all I had to do it with!'

*Mr. Herbert suggests that this book will be of most help to those who are having fairly good results in their own lives . . . but need to fine-tune what they are doing. He also suggests the book for those who are just starting out on their own as young adults. Although he does not mention it, **I also think this book could be a life saver for those whose lives have crashed and burned in some fundamental way . . . and want to clean up their act.***

As I finished the book, I was again reminded of the value of setting and pursuing worthwhile goals for ourselves. We can each do great things . . . if only we focus on doing so!"

Deatri King-Bey reviewer of RAWSISTAZ.com

*"How do I define my own personal success? What are the obstacles keeping me from succeeding? How do I get around, through, under, or over goal crushing obstacles? How do I start down the path of success? Is there a road map to help guide me down the road to success? **These are just a few of the questions answered in THE TWELVE UNIVERSAL LAWS OF SUCCESS by Herbert Harris.***

Using a combination of self-help concepts, biblical principles, and step-by-step procedures, Mr. Harris has written a well-organized, easy to understand guide to escort readers through the laws of success. Throughout each chapter, thought provoking questions are asked of the readers to help them focus on where they are, where they wish to go, and
how to get there.

Currently the target audience for this book is adults that are doing well in life but want to do better. I believe the primary target audience should be changed to teens and young adults. The first lesson Mr. Harris teaches is about poor self-image and how to overcome this barrier to success. The subsequent lessons are just as relevant to teens and young adult's lives. Why not teach young people how to succeed before they've been out in the world using the trial and error method.

Mr. Harris's no nonsense, cut to the chase approach in THE TWELVE UNIVERSAL LAWS OF SUCCESS made this an easy read that I believe many will find beneficial.
I even plan on having my teens work through the book as their summer project."